I0710799

KAREN KELLOCK 101

KAREN KELLOCK PH.D.

**Manual for
Superior Men**

**A complete theory based on Einstein physics,
Political Psychology, Systems Theory
and Archetypal Psychiatry.**

**FORMULA
All success attraction
All disease obstruction
All recovery elimination**

**You must fast on all three
OBSTRUCTIONS:
People
Habit
Food**

KAREN KELLOCK 101

SYSTEMS THEORY. The intricacies of systems affect all members and it means addiction/depression.   They're far more concerned with what people think than truth, and from that comes bedlam/ruin.   They make wrong decisions affecting other people based on flimsy or vile motives, many evil. We're to cover each other's faults but our sins are shouted from the rooftops by our spouses. The sins of the odd stranger are magnified, the sins of the conformist brother are taken in stride.

KAREN KELLOCK 101
Author Notes '23

GOD COMPLETES US
WE'RE MOLDED BY OUR GENERATION
TRENDS OF WOMEN HATE
FORGIVE AND THERE IS NO PAST
PERVERTED MALE CULTURE
PRAY TO FORGET IT ALL
SELFIX AND COMPLETION
THE CREATIVE ACT AND HARVEST

KAREN KELLOCK

101
SYSTEMS THEORY

Art and Science Discovery
www.karenkellock.org
see "Strips" of the Theory

KAREN KELLOCK

101

KAREN KELLOCK 101
Author Notes '23

GOD COMPLETES US

Just when I was losing my mind from the complexity and desire to be free, God completed me.

I never worked so hard in my life then suddenly the Great Work and Wonder was done, aye.

She was jealous of you, seeking to find fault. So she called em up and they filled her cup.

As Psalms says the kings collude together against the righteous. He is alone and it's treacherous.

Here I was just a renter in town but had to adapt to this high school atmosphere like I was owned.

The past doesn't exist so don't let em make you think it does. That's just a way to keep you down.

The past is just a dimension--way down the ladder of success vs. declension, so forget about it.

WE'RE MOLDED BY OUR GENERATION

People are molded by their generation. The older men just want younger women, so screw em.

If someone makes you that unhappy you gotta get rid of him honey. Don't be a dam masochist see.

Every story has bad times and a good ending. Stick on that now, forget the stuff at the beginning.

Author's Notes 2023

Unless you are like US you don't understand I guess. You just can't help but interrupt office.

You had to go thru a haze: a hellish Hades so to speak, an underworld you'll never again see.

Cher is a definite barrier breaker and that moves the dial for freedom to live without ridiculers.

TRENDS OF WOMEN HATE

There was a time men cherished women but then one generation started hating them.

I picked him, he did not choose me. And as a result I got him and my life went to hell quickly.

Eternity is forgiveness, forgiveness brings you to eternity. Grudges hook us in time/the temporary.

Ok so you go for younger women, fine. I'm not a younger woman so get out and goodbye.

I don't have to do what I've been doing for fifty years anymore: that is work, correct, explore.

I'm done. The Creative Act IS a structure in nature and it DOES have a beginning, middle and END.

I became sensitive to freeway sounds. The sounds of eternity with me rushing forward alone.

FORGIVE AND THERE IS NO PAST

Forgive, no past, everchanging places and spaces, living in eternity: that's where we need to be.

Forgive and there is no past. Hold grudges and it's like a dark shadow, depression/lack of success.

Author's Notes 2023

I'm done, I've completed the task God gave me to do. I ran the good race, I fought the good fight too.

I'm living in eternity with a cat on my desk. Turn off the phones and restrict all office access.

I felt invincible too when young, that they were always old. Traditional societies see the whole.

PERVERTED MALE CULTURE

Cruel society valued women for their youth and beauty and discarded them when they aged see.

That's the baby boomer view, but the new male likes the boss lady as he was used to that in mommy.

The young male LOVES meritocracy in a lady: You see proficiency and perspicacity is very sexy.

But not to older guys, they're molded differently. One asked for divorce when she got her Ph.D.

"He left me in other cities to hitchhike home. I grew paranoid of getting outa the car". Survivor

"He enjoyed humiliating me, he also loved standing me up just to show me who's who." Ex-love

Mom and dad I'm sorry I acted as I did. I was traumatized, out of control, an entitled twit.

It is perfectly understandable and predictable that you went crazy in that grenade range family.

You're perfectly happy and then someone starts chewing a bone and the day turns crappy.

You're perfectly happy and they arrive unannounced changing the rules of the game, trashed

Author's Notes 2023

If he just reminds you how old you are forget him now then see an exciting new world open up.

It's invasive immaturity you can't stand and that's why you're a lifelong recluse man: privacy, amen.

PRAY TO FORGET IT ALL

Please Father let me forget it all. The humiliations, being used by evil men without protection.

And then being blamed all over town as if I was the bad one. Always the two tiered justice system.

It was terrifying living in the land of accusation. Mixed signals, whisperings, killing my reputation.

And don't be putting people on a pedestal. Worship the right one: it's GOD and that's ALL.

You gonna just leave me here? I imposed on you so much I got used to it dear. Frenemy

No you're not funny nor deep but you think you are and I guess that's all that matters for now.

Don't ruin your looks & attractiveness by worrying about the future. Love this minute sister.

Today I reached a major milestone in life called Completion of the Creative Act/I'm high.

In a life of competitions and comparisons you may lose your magnetism and the self be nothing.

SELFIX AND COMPLETION

Completion of a Creative Act acts as as kernel of attraction to the means of earthly production.

Author's Notes 2023

With completion I feel an ocean going through my veins. It snowed, I hear the wind, I love the rains.

I've so joyously and exuberantly elated that I'm finished I could yell in gaiety for eternity: riches

I need office hours where I'm not interrupted EVER and I KNOW that otherwise it's a mental HAZARD.

I'm done, people, I'm done. It took fifty years but I don't expect you to understand the pain & tears.

Of course we're gonna age and die, I mean wake up. They act like it's a disease so get hep.

The generations come in and go out together. That's the whole life vision as you rise higher.

THE CREATIVE ACT AND HARVEST

I felt I was being carried along in a stream in spite of myself. It's the creative act: HARVEST.

I'm celebrating and I'm retiring. That's the party after a life of fruitless striving/nasty fighting.

As an older woman I'm not looking for a young man just enjoying the moment, that's where it's at.

I'm so tired after giving birth to the Creative Act. I just wanna rest now and enjoy the minutes.

I'm retired, I wanna enjoy the moment now. Not even the news except a few good shows.

I just wanna enjoy the moment now so the best way you can love me is to just leave me alone.

I did the task God gave me to do and I fought the good fight. I just wanna enjoy the moment now/bye.

Author's Notes 2023

See that break in the clouds, that fascinates me now. So little time/so much to enjoy around.

Have a nice life. Get food, clean house, take care of pets and be nice then one day you die.

You're done, now the fun starts. To enjoy the fruits of your labor all these years, loving the perks.

KAREN KELLOCK 101

SUCCESS VS. LOSERS [SIMPLE PRINCIPAL]
HISTORY FROM EARLIEST TRAUMA
LAYERS OF STRESS BECOMES MENTAL ILLNESS
GOSSIPING AND CALUMNY IS TREACHERY
SOUL MURDER BY SIBLINGS
YOUNG WOMEN ARE IMPOSED ON
FLIP FLOPS: SUDDEN REALITY SWITCHES
SHIRK SHUNNING
RICH LIBERAL TYRANTS AND SNOBS
THE EXALTED BECOME THE WORST
WITHOUT GOD THE ENEMY TAKES OVER
GOD RESTORED ME DOUBLE FOR MY TROUBLE
LOOK AT ME: I'VE BEEN HURT
STRANGER IN A STRANGE LAND/UNWANTED, UNLOVED
SNOWBALL EFFECT IN DEVELOPMENTAL PSYCHOLOGY
HOMELESS, FENCELESS, DEFENSELESS
THE WHOLE GENERATION IS LIKE THIS
THE GOLDEN GIRLS WRECKED CULTURE
OLDER WOMEN SHOULD BE EXEMPLARS
ABSOLUTE CHASTITY OR CHEAP?
OPEN BORDERS VS. GENIUS' FEW FRIENDS
AFTER GOING THROUGH ALL THAT...
SELF-DEFINE BY ALL THINGS
WOMEN BELONG IN THE HOME
SAINTS SHOW SUCCESSIVE RENUNCIATIONS
ALCOHOL: THE END OF IT ALL
WHOREMONGERS AND GOSSIPS
SLUTS ARE DEMONS
STUCK IN RUTS
COMPUTERS ARE TERRIBLE TIME WASTERS
BUT GOD!
OUR SINS STAND OUT/THERES ARE IGNORED
WE'RE TOLD TO CAST DOWN WRONG THOUGHTS
MUST GET A FRESH START
SLAVE TO YOUR THOUGHTS
WAKING UP DISTRAUGHT
YOU FAIL CUZ YOU'RE MAD AS HELL
WOMEN SEEK APPROVAL THRU TRADITION

KAREN KELLOCK 101

DEVELOPING A PRICKLY CRUST
CONTROLLED BY LIBERAL HARRIDANS
ANSWER COMES BEFORE THE PROBLEM
CONTROLLING THOUGHTS
BE NOT AFRAID OF CHANGE
GOD'S SOLUTIONS ARE ALWAYS SO CLEVER
CURE THE MIND THRU OLD MOVIES: MENTAL TRANSPORT
DUNNING KRUGER IS IN EFFECT
PREVALENT AGEISM
SAGACITY IS SICK OF THEIR PROJECTIONS
RETIRE TO AVOID AGEISM
GREATEST VALUE: INDEPENDENCE
USELESS DEBATES WITH MENTAL MIDGETS
SECRET ALLIANCES AND TRIANGULATIONS
THEY MISTREAT YOU, GOD PROMOTES YOU
SMALL TOWN POLITIX
NEVER COMPLAIN, NEVER EXPLAIN
WE MISS YOU HARRY
FORGIVE FEMINIST MOTHER TO MATURE
WAIT FOR DUST TO SETTLE
ZEZEBEL IS A TALKER
WITH JUST A KEYBOARD AND ROCKS
THE LEFT LOVES THE CHICOMS
HAVE BORDERS OR BE TAKEN OVER
GOING BACK IS SWIMMING UPSTREAM IN MUD
WATCH THE MERE CONTACT
THE OTHER DIRECTED ARE MENTALLY EFFECTED
THEY SAID IT COULDN'T BE DONE
DOUBLE FOR YOUR TROUBLE
NARCISSISTS GO BY THEIR FEELINGS
NARCISSISTS SEE PEOPLE AS TOOLS
DRAWN TO BAD BOYS/WILD GIRLS
HOLLYWOOD, BIG PHARMA, GLOBALISTS
BETRAYALS IN TRADITIONS
CUCKHOLDED BETA "MALE FEMINISTS"
TESTED AND TRIED THEN THE PRIZE
AVOID ALL EVIL HELPERS

KAREN KELLOCK 101

PEOPLE ARE THE ENVIRONMENT
SHOCKING INSIGHT: HERD IS POWER
MORE VICTIMIZED, MORE FAVOR LATER
JESUS HAS THE SOLUTION BEFORE THE PROBLEM
GUTS FULL OF FIBER
DREAMING OF POT ROAST AND GRAVY
MEAT-AVERSION: IS IT BIBLICAL?
VEGANISM: MENTAL ILLNESS BLOCKS CURE?
INSTANT ENERGY WITH FIRST STEAK?
STOP PUTTING DOWN SMOOTHIES
FIFTIES EATING IS BEST LOOKING
EAT WHAT YOU WANT BUT FAST THEN CHOOSE UP
REVERSAL DIETING OF PALEO FOODS
MEAT-ONLY FOR IMMUNE HEALING?
THE ROAST EXPERIMENT/JUST CAN'T DO IT
TROPICAL DIET: FRUIT, COCONUT, PORK
"FRUGI-CARNIVORES"
BORN TO BE A MEAT-ABSTAINER
HEARTBURN FROM NON-FRUITS
MODERN FRUITARIANS ARE GLUTTONS
LACTO-FRUITARIANISM: FRUIT AND CHEESE
NOT GONNA FORCE FEED THE MEAT
THE PROBLEM IS ACID: ERHET
ICE CREAM CHEMICAL DESTRUCTION
DIETARY SEEKING, WILL IT EVER END?
SECRET TO LONGEVITY: AVOID PEOPLE
STICKY FINGER HOUSEKEEPERS
THE CREATIVE ACT AND COMPLETION
CREATIVE ACT IS PLANNED PLUS LINK
SHAME IS THE RESULT OF TWO THINGS
MENTAL TYRANNY
RETIRE TO THE RIGHT BRAIN
GOD IS ETERNITY NOT THE TEMPORARY
GOD ISN'T A CLOUD WITHOUT RAIN
WHY FEAR IF YOU'RE WITH GOD?
LUCRATIVE HUNCH OR HATE THEIR GUTS?
ESCAPE SYSTEM CRUTCHES
FULFILL DESTINY OR MISS IT ENTIRELY

KAREN KELLOCK 101:

SYSTEMS THEORY

LAYERS OF STRESS BECOMES MENTAL ILLNESS

Having temporary mental illness from stress or layers is an opportunity to see how people treat us.

I had felt SO much stress and SO much blatant betrayal ALL AT ONCE that = I was insane.

Layers upon layers, breaking points, step functions, group tyranny, mis-accusations: it adds up hon.

They were so cruel it's hard to even conceive it. All from social hypnosis and having silly fits.

They're far more concerned with what people think than truth, and from that comes bedlam/ruin.

They make wrong decisions affecting other people based on flimsy or vile motives, many evil.

And of course family [hix politix] enters in and that's about jealousy triangles or a similar hex.

Cover a person's faults, you're on God's side. Expose and discredit em, you're on the wrong side.

"Touch not my anointed". Tho' Noah was drunk he was anointed--we make mistakes and God knows it.

GOSSIPING AND CALUMNY IS TREACHERY

We're to cover each other's faults--but our sins are shouted from the rooftops by our spouses.

Mother and sisters gossiped about every little thing to perfect strangers and I was thus sequestered.

They were compelled to bring me down and keep me there. That was my sisters and mother, I swear.

The sins of the odd stranger are magnified, the sins of the conformist brother are taken in stride.

Touch not My anointed means: stop gossiping/sowing discord about My children or I'll be in it.

It doesn't matter WHAT the accepted do, it's ok, but anything the peculiar does is put on display.

God will deal with the troublemakers. Now don't get all worked up but wait and watch God erupt.

Stay in peace, God sees what's happening. He will not let a sower of discord prevail happily.

No worries, once God vindicates He'll take you to fresh breaks and higher levels than these fakes.

The fake friend gets you riled up fighting useless battles then sowing discord with the rabble.

I can't stop you from sowing discord but I can escape by knowing that God abhors it.

CALUMNY: murdering a person's reputation with the folks. God hates this and will get you jerks.

KAREN KELLOCK 101

You told em I did things that I never even heard of--you're so outrageous and ridiculous, my sista!

SOUL MURDER BY SIBLINGS

Two liberal feminists ruined by college came home to destroy their little sister a Christian conservative.

It's the siblings who murder souls since we self-identify against the ground of lesser roles.

If I see you garrulously clowning with jocularity with the multitudes baby I'll say goodbye today.

Cuz what about me--you don't care about ME? Am I equal to the herd in your social promiscuity?

I'm number ONE to you or you won't see me at all. Bye y'all.

Life's a hierarchy. It's an insult to put Jesus on same level with Krishna, Vishnu and Buddha ya know?

And I'm not gonna compete with your millions of acquaintances that mean nothing, good grief.

Michelle did that--she would bring over all these people! Like bringing flowers, a book, a table.

You are socially promiscuous so you can appear to have "friends" cuz that's the in thing, not genius.

So you're all thrown in together and it's boring, loud and chaotic and I've had enough of it.

I asked you not to bring friends and you did it anyway cuz it's second nature to you to be that way.

I have my OWN friends and I vet my OWN houseguests but that's hateful to these pests.

Even in locked condo buildings they'd get to me, only marriage saved me from these creeps.

YOUNG WOMEN ARE IMPOSED ON

A single woman has a friggin' bull's eye painted on her and nothing will stop em but her new Sir.

I was mighty good-lookin' at 25 and I can attest I wanted to enter a monastery just to survive.

And men in power--Ph.D. sponsors and the like--were the worst, compelled to impose and flirt.

Well with all this I caved in. I lost my identity and became mousy, nondescript, lost, no friends.

The Fallen Hero Syndrome: increasing betrayals as you spiral down/all support is lost for the clown.

People who were your friends and brethren turn their heel against you and it's always unbelievable.

As I spiraled down without support/energy to stop it my spouse shouted my sins from the rooftops.

He's my ex and dead as heck cuz God HATES this and has said as much, so look up and be led.

I was a very sick sinner but still anointed--can you believe this about our divine appointment?

The bleakest era of my life was drinking AT situations, this ruined my health and created strife.

NO alcohol whatsoever cuz the mere ATOM changes the matrix and you're a nobody and unclever.

Every time I drank it all went to hell suddenly. Success also happens suddenly, that's our Daddy.

KAREN KELLOCK 101

With the Fallen Hero Syndrome your biggest fans can become your cruelest foes when let down.

Marriage is absolute freedom for a woman. Finally protected she can flourish in a stable environment.

FLIP FLOPS: SUDDEN REALITY SWITCHES

They say obscene and cruel things to be part of the club. It's so embarrassing--please grow up!

How much mental illness comes from our split or bifurcation, mal-adapting to their flip-flops.

Most mental illness comes from our bifurcation [SPLIT] from mal-adapting to their flips.

Our flip flops are intertwined and timed with theirs and that's the contagion of lunacy right there.

Our flip flops are a mal-adaptation to their flip-flops and later those systems we recreate.

You expect it, you bring it on. That's the whole sick cycle perpetuating itself until we're done.

I was so split I didn't see the disrespect then I'd swing into forced "high self esteem" effects.

With trauma we park there: we make a template of the situation which we recreate in the future.

I may have lacked empathy and compassion but after going through all that I feel for all of them.

Predictably, it's the women who perpetrate FGM and all other "honor systems" of abuse, here too.

SHIRK SHUNNING

KAREN KELLOCK 101

Liberals are more interested in protecting illegals from ICE than their own citizens from vice.

Either be a senior member of the royal family or a jet-guzzling celebrity preaching on whatever.

In Hollywood they all wanna be the "cool kid". Look at me man, I hate Donald Trump that shit.

They're totally coddled, surrounded by a team telling em everything they do is righteous, right-on.

Hollywood scum don't watch true news/don't know what they're saying so they're easily EXPOSED.

After years of secret meetings and black-listings celebrities are exposing it so see these.

Shunning is a form of honor violence. It's not for sins but just refusing to conform brings a sentence.

SUCCESS VS. LOSERS [SIMPLE PRINCIPAL]

We all had to start somewhere on the way up but the difference is success people USE it all.

They don't park at/whine about the past they use all they've learned from it for giant world success.

Use everything bad that happened to your advantage and use it to help others manage.

You need to SEE something as a tool to get you where you belong and to the past, so long.

The successful all say: the bad stuff that happened in their life got em to where they are today.

When looking at the past do you see a bad situation or a TOOL and an incredible opportunity?

KAREN KELLOCK 101

If alcohol's involved that's a cold-blooded switch and automatically perceived rejection.

In **RECOVER** from all this, do something good with your [justified] anger.

HISTORY FROM EARLIEST TRAUMA

God wants us to have a fresh start. But they don't want us to have this so they muddy our aura

As trauma is embedded in layers and pain is deeper, being totally insane is how we appear.

To add alcohol to that fiery mix you have prison material as you can see in lives of convicts.

All that pain made you adapt in a certain way and build a certain muscle you'll need some day.

I built a social muscle of avoidance, distance and aristocratic reserve of the nonconformist.

Every bad thing can be turned around as your opportunity for good and helping others, understood?

YOU NEVER LOST IT but you had caved into their abuse and that was it, but now you're back.

The modern church is about being good yet Jesus said "Don't call me good, only God is good", not the Pharisees' "shoulds".

Living in a shack was my lesson and when I learned it sufficiently God took me to my mansion.

People you talk to are the environment you adapt to--they can make you tired or energize you.

RICH LIBERAL TYRANTS AND SNOBS

So now you can see what I'm talking about. It was rough--**REALLY** rough-- having to suck up.

For these dark cowards had a GLEAMING image to the world like the biblical Pharisees of old.

They were affluent/protected liberals who wanna take our guns and throw us to the wolves!

They are rich, entitled, coddled and surrounded by go-fers on government pensions galore.

Rich, entitled and don't know what they're talking about--embarrassingly ignorant like CNN.

They totally go along with whatever narrative to stay in the in-club and to the right they scoff/snub.

The first thing authoritarians do is put you in data bases, then gulags, then death camps.

Authoritarians always use force to dominate a population so they always come for the guns.

Take the guns and we're totally dependent on the state and at the mercy of common criminals.

Disarmed nations have an exploding crime rate hundreds of times more than the armed U.S.

The Third World is being used to bring down the west. It's all been planned and announced.

You're not allowed to stand your ground against anyone endorsed by the globalists.

THE EXALTED BECOME THE WORST

Does all strange behavior come down to grooves? I think so, they're called "autonomisms" too.

Something happened being paired with a stimulus and it was a groove from then on: cue, trigger.

And then with layers from the years of reactions and counter-reactions you have a locked dominion.

Something would trigger the two-against-one feeing of triangulation-suffocation and I'd relapse.

When a high-powered, exalted God-loving and energetic being goes berserk he's the worst.

Especially feeling a victim of all those twits? That was a long long time ago, how'd I know it.

I was weakened because God withdrew His power and the holy spirit ceased to strive with me.

In the twinkling of an eye, gone was all my vision, power, understanding, intellect, reason or will.

I learned in this sudden deflation that it was God's power upholding me, not little ol' me.

WITHOUT GOD THE ENEMY TAKES OVER

Without God you have no power to withstand the enemy and your hedge of protection is cast away.

If you confirm these people, if you let them in you're showing who you are as stupid, dense and evil.

We live in an era of pedophiles, Satan worshippers and baby-killers—women bragging afterwards.

These people are so disgusting it's hard to imagine. We're sinking to the lower limits and it's hellish.

By your loving hospitality you show only your dense loyalty to a stupid narrative of liberal treachery.

My past is ever-with me, keeping me humble and making me distance myself from the rabble.

You were a fool many times over with that creep--its the early trauma wanting correction, peeps.

My law: I don't want to adapt to anything and I don't want anything imposed on me at all.

As I unpeel back I'm in Junior High playing trumpet then getting involved with boys I'll bet.

The more I divorce from it the more God can bless it I guess.

GOD RESTORED ME DOUBLE FOR MY TROUBLE

The less you seek human help the more God will pull you up cuz you're relying just on Him, yah.

The Lord will bring out the books, not man. He's too stupid to understand em but God has a plan.

They shun you now, you shun em back when you're famous, fabulously rich and renowned.

Forgive em but baby never take em back cuz they shunned and from this you're on the run!

God blesses people for their faith by giving them more than they had before-- He RESTORES.

Prisoners of hope: Today I'm returning double your former prosperity as the firstborn of the nations. Zech 9: 9-13

He stores our tears in a bottle and records all of our sorrows. Psalms 56: 8

So horrible, so painful and unfair--but it all made you the person that you are, a star.

So much destruction and loss brought compassion for the people who are hurting and lost.

KAREN KELLOCK 101

No evidence of smoke after the fiery furnace--there is **NO EVIDENCE** of our past sins and disgrace.

Stop dragging around your ashes. Give em up and get beauty instead--this works like magic.

You can't keep the old stuff and get the new stuff. You can't maintain a bad attitude or bluff.

The things that hurt become our identity like a badge we wear and it's counterproductive and petty.

LOOK AT ME: I'VE BEEN HURT

"Look at me, I've been hurt" should be replaced by "look at me, I've been healed".

Although my father and mother hath forsaken me yet the Lord takes me up/adopts me as His own.

Grew up feeling terrible like it was all my fault then God chose me as apple of His eye, an elf.

Feel differently about yourself as God's little elf and the things inside will blossom and come out.

I felt like no one knew I existed or paid attention until I realized God attends to ALL my needs man.

STRANGER IN A STRANGE LAND/UNWANTED, UNLOVED

I felt like a stranger in a strange land until I realized God owns the whole thing and He's my fan.

You get so hurt in one area and under so much stress you think everyone's a terrible pest.

The need to belong is so strong that rejection brings massive stress and we look it, a mess.

You can't make everyone else pay for what a few did way back in the day but is that you today?

Yes we want justice [MAKE SOMEONE PAY] but God is our Vindicator so happily wait for Him today.

Friend, don't waste one more day of your now or your future grieving those sad past years.

Sweetie you ARE due something from all of that, but our God is the One who will pay you back.

The wounded may try to collect from everyone else, driving em away forever and staying lost.

God can take the wounded and make things better than they woulda been had it never happened.

There are then two kinds of pain: the pain of change and the much worse pain of staying the same.

Doorways of pain that lead to bondage: I got thru this, now that, now bound in a bad marriage.

There were layers of pain and somewhere in all that the doors closed on my heart, just sayin'

With every new reactionary pain a door closed on my heart until I felt soul murdered for a start.

Early trauma = beaten by teens in park = started drinking = bad marriage = doors closed on heart.

SNOWBALL EFFECT IN DEVELOPMENTAL PSYCHOLOGY

It's a snowball effect in developmental psychology: First this, then that, then it all goes splat.

Early trauma with momma, began drinking at 15, married an alki, escaped into decades of misery.

KAREN KELLOCK 101

I splashed into the desert and was so worn out my maxed-out emotions exploded and blew up.

Once you're hurt you gotta bull's eye painted on you and the men smell blood/treat you like dirt.

Once you're hurt women take shots cuz you're degraded--your appearance triggers targeting.

I wasn't a classist and never mentioned my Ph.D. cuz we're "all one/equal" I was told--aren't we?

A protected home with a fence vs. exposed in a small down full of the angry, envious and dense.

HOMELESS, FENCELESS, DEFENSELESS

Dear Lord, we couldn't have been more different. But I had to learn this the hard way, amen.

Home and a fence: It's just your thing and everyone there has been vetted and very extra-nice.

To not have a wall is racist. Blacks suffer the most but open borders advocates don't care about this.

Homeless, fenceless, exposed to the masses: My God, there is nothing on this earth worse.

I could name names but these guys are in their fifties now with families, sure they never think of me.

The issue is: it's not about taking vengeance on the culprits cuz the whole generation is like this.

Women are hateful to each other in this "feminist" climate cuz competition is our thing mate.

In pre-feminist generations the women were KIND and sweet to each other, treated like sisters.

KAREN KELLOCK 101

Tenderness, the female virtue: They don't even know what tender means anymore, PEE-YOU.

It's all about getting THEIR rights and needs met--but that's not what the female is all about.

Female Power is about Leading thru Serving. It's actually the Christ model they're destroying.

I'd get into crying jags and maudlin scenes as the ego-alien material rose up, so unclean.

THE WHOLE GENERATION IS LIKE THIS

You see crying jags in mental hospitals, deep and sick things in childhood never resolved at all.

Crying jags, drunken days to "repair", terrified of bad image, being called insane or can't manage.

I had been so badly misjudged by lowminds but was in no condition to defend myself and blind.

Then the whole town or clan pegs you and getting back up takes a miracle or years of looking up.

It's not about "feminism" but right and wrong. Pre-feminist ladies: nice to each other all along.

The petty competition and sterile dynasties of the feminist world comes from evil and wrong.

It's whatever works for power: If it's TWO against ONE that dyad never changes/stays sour.

The scary selfish feminist I've described is an evil thing though they virtue-signal day and night.

The female is to be dreamy-eyed and yes, we cry. Not focused, angry, vindictive with LIES.

It took me 30 years to clearly see everything she said and did to me cuz I wanted acceptance, see?

THE GOLDEN GIRLS WRECKED CULTURE

It was the Golden Girls who changed culture not the later sitcoms which were much nastier.

How many feeble-minded socially hypnotized women copied Blanche's sluttiness portrayed as "cute"?

The older woman is supposed to ELEVATE the morals of youth, not be the worst of the uncouth.

I personally knew a woman mimicking "Blanche" as the biggest slut in town, like wearing a crown.

Bathroom humor and sluttiness portrayed as cute and superior--these are globalists motives ulterior.

Golden Girls: screamingly funny on the outer while the inner goes to hell with suggestions subliminal.

It's much more dangerous than nastier shows since older women [grandma] are so in the know?

Are we supposed to emulate old women who are dirty and nasty but dressed in clothes so classy?

The mentally effete also have dirty minds. If you love dogs they accuse you of bestiality, so unkind!

OLDER WOMEN SHOULD BE EXEMPLARS

No--the older woman is an EXEMPLAR of the higher and when they go lower it's DISASTER.

Women cozy up to Big Daddy: Big GOV, tradition, social hypnosis and the herd: being catty.

KAREN KELLOCK 101

Elizabeth Warren is a socialist, can't you see this? Promising things, sowing discord, always pissed.

I don't know what I'd do without Joyce, she's helped me so much. Heretic? No a friend I can trust.

The psychological reaction to misfitting the system is **SHAME** then they all pile on to increase blame.

Shame from misfitting denses the aura to a muddy color and now you've lost all your charisma.

A woman is admired most but obscenities or taking the Lord's name in vain leads to sudden disgust.

Letting go of the old [dissipative structures] allows us to have more creativity and security in the future.

Please stop talking about age. I'm gonna live until the moment I die and my creativity won't change.

Since feelings vacillate all I can do is trust what I know/stick to that and ignore feelings like hate.

We gotta watch our feelings. Stick to the facts and reason or you have **NO** anchor just rancor.

ABSOLUTE CHASTITY OR CHEAP?

NEVER trust your feelings when it comes to men. Stay a good moral woman and **NEVER** give in.

Cuz you'll be **HURT**, ok? Casual sex means: cast aside, replaced or minimized in some way.

Never think it's expected cuz "everyone does it" or you'll sink your own ship and then be rejected.

Whenever you feel that "pull" like it's expected or you're defective, stop and take a deep breath.

If you're a Christian wife you are told to love your husband even though you may hate him.

And as you love him and respect him he trusts you and that is necessary for love to occur.

How can a man trust a woman who is acting like that, saying those things, being so rinky-dink?

I grew so terrified of the things Cindy would say. I already knew she was on the horn all day.

Good Lord women can be cruel. When the need to push you down is that strong, cunning mules.

Women are supposed to be sweet little ladies, not all this stuff shady but also rinky-dink and cheesy.

What has inferiorized the female? Feminist ideas so stale, standing up to the male, being for sale.

What has inferiorized the female? Feminist ideas so stale, rising up against the male, being for sale.

OPEN BORDERS VS. GENIUS' FEW FRIENDS

How can a man love she who wants open borders, destroying jobs and the country he loves?

Open borders in the home too--people interrupting, coming and going like Grand Central Station.

Ever since "Friends" on TV people think they're superior to have loud crowds around, see?

But Maslow has proven the mentally healthy and genius have very FEW friends, really.

People talk too much about sex and "performance". Before, sex was private/sacred tho' important.

KAREN KELLOCK 101

"They make it as commonplace and mechanical as going to the bathroom".
Marion Kellock

The higher the ORDER the more DISGUST and need for a BORDER as I found out, over and over.

At about age 24 another archetype took over and she was another person altogether.

Honeytrap: Using beautiful women to lure rich men into compromising situations and record em.

This is the declension: Young girl has premarital sex, demons enter and now her archetype is wrecked.

Demons enter through sexual connection and that's why the slut/whoremonger is a haunted house.

It's like God pushes our frustration, jealousy and envy buttons until we become saints.

AFTER GOING THROUGH ALL THAT...

Depression, anxiety and panic attacks are not signs of weakness but exhaustion after all that.

After trying to remain strong for so long, panic attacks are a warning after exhaustion.

Panic Attacks feel like HEART attacks and that's why they cause such panic but it's just a mimic.

After going thru all that and layers of abuse/shame buildup you may start looking like a lunatic.

The Adam and Eve Syndrome: He worships her as God then when she leaves he's lost his soul.

Key to longevity: avoid people, they'll only take you down a rat hole.

KAREN KELLOCK 101

In the late stages of a society bizarre behavior proliferates and is accepted as all-ok.

Pedophilia is not a sexual orientation, it's a predatory sickness but the left normalizes rape and abuse.

SELF-DEFINE BY ALL THINGS

Self-define thru your acts. Do you clean house, keep early nights, always feed your dogs and cats?

Notice great things about you and all you've achieved--let those define you not the creeps.

My dogs and cats know for sure I'll always feed em on time because that's how I'm self-defined.

Not just obvious achievements and degrees but the LITTLE things--the insignificant to please.

WOMEN BELONG IN THE HOME

Of course I wanna stay home. Here it's beauty and magic but out there its a mass of syndromes.

Of course I call myself a "shut-in". Then I don't have to leave home and it stops your arguin'.

HOME is joy, magic, beauty, fascination, everything at hand. OUT is chemicals, zombies and tedium.

My timid 10-year old cat finally stood up to the dog and she obviously feels so much power now.

So many nooks, crannies and views to explore in my lovely home so filled with happiness galore.

Feminists see homelife as imprisonment but I say this woman belongs in the home, amen.

KAREN KELLOCK 101

The internet is INFINITE so why stay on any part of it out of habit? Keep exploring, MOVE it...

If you wanna see me you gotta come here on my turf. I go nowhere, I'm a shut-in remember.

SAINTS SHOW SUCCESSIVE RENUNCIATIONS

The saints' lives show successive renunciations of one thing too constricting after another.

I wanna maximize my day: I don't wanna adapt to anything nor have anything imposed on me.

That means to eat dessert first and dance now--to cut away the dead wood and move ahead.

We need to be rich, that's our only hedge.

For everything there is an appointed time, an appropriate time for everything on earth. Eccl 3: 1

The system may be keeping you down but so what, there's always a crack to break thru that.

Now that I'm done with this Great Work gonna open up to the environment, family and neighborhood.

Open up to synchronicity IN SITU--in your situation. Can't do that on the computer time wastin'

I keep trying to get something outa the PC but can't--will return to TRUE reality for enchantment.

Just because I got something outa two videos I kept trying for years but it's just emptiness, you know?

ALCOHOL: THE END OF IT ALL

Enlightened genius coming thru when sober but with ONE atom of drink I was nothing but a loser.

Researched my Scottish roots: They were either great famous orators or died of drink in gutter.
There's no in-between: with Indians or other sensitives it's not one atom, that's the facts hon'

Alcohol is a conduit to devil and his demons--it's embarrassing waking up to our fall/being less than.

A little herb if you need something but it tears up the lungs/some experience psychosis with edibles.

I needed the herb all those years to constantly resolve contradiction and manage impositions.

Don't ever let em in your home cuz they'll rise up against you and take over--NEVER.

WHOREMONGERS AND GOSSIPS

They will use you for sex and take your money too. Get wise, be chaste, love God and don't be a fool.

You continue to gossip and tear down like you do, get ready for a visitation as God fights you.

I did nothing to deserve calumnious officious gossip from you girls. You are jealous, envious retards.

You're to chum up to people easily and that's being "social" so alcohol is a social lubricant/pleasing.

Had to get drunk before any social event. 50% of females are alcoholic, these stats are definite.

If you gotta be drunk to enjoy these people there's something wrong. Boring, mediocre throng.

Sheba, biblical troublemaker: God dwelt with him as his lifeless body was thrown over the wall.

While Miriam was criticizing Moses suddenly her skin became full of leprosy--God hates this you see.

SLUTS ARE DEMONS

Women: If you have a slutty friend get ready for the Jezebel Spirit to rise up/not "cute" like Blanche.

For the slut is a demon and it's cunningly intrusive in other insidious ways you can't be predictin'

I had a friend who was always sowing discord on my behalf and it ended up so expensive, my gosh.

The slut demon is a reaction to the discord demon cuz a weak woman feels it's her only protection.

Golden Girls: Dumb was cute, the old one too, Dorothy a shrew but Blanch [slut] was most cool.

This had a wild but subtle influence on the whole era--old ladies acting brazen then see ya.

Women thinking they're cool talking crap and making lewd jokes is so unwholesome and evil folks.

A slut demon will start imposing on you in other ways, even stealing and even your spouse, ok?

I hear old women taking the Lord's name in vain, I see them tolerating sin/pornography all day.

I hear them gossiping at lunch "How'd she get that money?" and other officious words so catty.

Or making remarks about age--that's another mean thing they do as if you're expendable too.

STUCK IN RUTS

KAREN KELLOCK 101

Get stuck in ruts--like keep watching the same video to fill time not hobbies/projects which are so fine.

Or preaching to the choir: watching videos you already know. Don't do this--get back in the flow!

I'm NOT gonna watch TV all day but how's that different from a PC? GET REAL, it's not ok.

Not gonna waste my life on a computer. Sounds so intelligent doesn't it, but it's a TV and no better.

Gonna go back into the right-brain, how I was in the desert wilderness--loving stars, sun, even the rain.

COMPUTERS ARE TERRIBLE TIME WASTERS

How can I enjoy synchronicity if I'm sitting here trying to get something from the stupid PC?

Repetition or empty chants is from emptiness.

From midnight until 6 pm. I'm sitting here making it my whole life, fun, study and career.

Well goodbye joker you're been a distraction from home, family, pets, God, the yard and neighbors.

I'll just get the headlines from now on. They change constantly and will be irrelevant where I'm goin'

Successful people know 99% didn't work but then one thing did and since then they were rich.

When you start researching junior high sweethearts you know you're missing it--get a fresh start.

To let the past go, think of death--of flying off to eternity where there's no memory of it.

KAREN KELLOCK 101

That embarrassing event you ruminate about will not exist in eternity, you'll have no memory of it.

To erase those embarrassing, humiliating, painful or hurtful memories, simply LIVE IN ETERNITY.

Imagine yourself flying around heaven, looking back at this ball of mud but you can't remember it.

Much memory is distorted--it's not the event but the REACTIONS of others in a system that warps it.

They're doing ridiculous things all the time but since they "fit" no one sees or makes remarks, ya think?

Just gonna use the computer as a tool for my own work but not take on the news/dirty world.

BUT GOD!

They so minimize sin they think we should take em back with their mere silly apology.

God said I didn't create you to fight but to write. Don't respond anymore, stay HIGH.

No watered down chaff I want hellfire sin-and-repentance, hell-and-heaven preaching

Every writer wants to be read or why else would they be doing it? There'd be no reason for it.

Though the devil thought he was winning he just ended up equipping me to facilitate learning.

OUR SINS STAND OUT/THERES ARE IGNORED

Everyone's a sinner but the sins of the nonconformist stand out more while the others are ignored.

KAREN KELLOCK 101

God said: All that willful effort--now cast your care on me to take it, enjoy now leisure genius.

Unique ideas from a lifetime of hell mal-adapting to other people which is an enigma as well.

I just always wanted to get back to my room. Either it's boring or I feel imposed on, in a fume.

You're so good that someone will want to bring you up. it's called the Miracle of the Money Bags.

I'm waiting for that ONE. It's a case of there's only one right link and infinite of wrong or dumb.

The mere fact they think like they do indicates they're arrogant, so don't respond back.

You can't have an obedient life without an obedient thought life. Joyce Meyer

WE'RE TOLD TO CAST DOWN WRONG THOUGHTS

You didn't know you could cast down wrong thoughts or shut your mind against such?

Instead of taking every ornery thought in your head and taking it as your own/rolling it around?

Waking up depressed shall not stand because the joy of the Lord is my strength.

Listen to Satan's injected thoughts will keep you from God's plan for your life--they're rot!

Satan's favorite thing is to tell me I'm no good and should be ashamed--that was my whole thing.

Shame is the biggest indicator of the bulimic. It so wrecks her thoughts she can't stop it.

MUST GET A FRESH START

You've made too big of mistakes, your life is over, you 'll never get over the past. Satan
No one cares about you, you won't get the job, you're a failure for life. More from Satan

Everything with Satan is "ever" and "never"--it's never gonna change/you'll always fail, whatever.

Bear in mind His commandments then you'll be able to practice them: it's the same system.

My mind would go back into hellish misery from the past and I'd get into every detail of the mess.

Shame, guilt and anger thinking about what happened while the future goes blank/darkens.

Through the word we keep our mind renewed, know what to do, bash wrong thoughts too/soon.

If you make your mind up and ask God to help you it's like a steel trap against the foe's crap.

We don't "think" thoughts we "choose" em as they stream by. Don't be a fool, tell em all goodbye.

SLAVE TO YOUR THOUGHTS

Satan wants to wreck my future and He knows how: just get me thinking about him or her.

I was a slave to my thoughts and always mad as they triggered resentments until this was my focus.

Once I saw it's Satan bringing this painful shame and resentment I was able to turn it off in a minute.

Once with God no one can stop you BUT you must set your mind in the right direction or stop it.

Every embarrassing faux paux Satan would bring to mind just as I embarked on good thoughts.

I just wanted peace of mind but couldn't achieve it through any pills, potions, booze I could find.

The heroine addict taking drugs to shut the mind up doesn't understand these EASY principals of God.

Watch your thoughts. When something noxious comes up you'll know what to do: throw em out!

Stop thinking they're your own and know who's putting em in there--then no more problem.

WAKING UP DISTRAUGHT

I had such a problem with these thoughts I'd wake up distraught and go to bed angry at y'all.

The level of my failure was always equal to the intensity of whoever I was mad at, see?

I'd remember stupid things I did and flush with embarrassment as if it just happened.

I'd remember antics of my youth from the vantage point of an adult and STING with regret.

Well God doesn't want us to STING. We're supposed to give it all to Jesus, let HIM carry this thing.

Fantasies, thoughts and constructions die with us--toxic burdens are no more thank goodness.

God can help you renew your mind but it doesn't happen overnight--just start thinking right.

It's an aged groove--you can't have wrong thoughts for 40 years and suddenly it all runs smooth.

You wonder why everything's not different in your life--it's because a mental change takes time.

After you've changed thoughts you must also KEEP the victory--we GAIN then we MAINTAIN.

YOU FAIL CUZ YOU'RE MAD AS HELL

Must be diligent of thoughts every hour since Satan roams around like a lion seeking to devour.

It takes up so much energy to go back/through it all the future is completely wrecked, that's all.

A peaceful mind is what we want: "Well I can't help it I'm just a worrier" is what I'm talking about.

A PEACEFUL mind: God wants us to have leisure cuz it's true what they say about the work grind.

No "I can't help it" cuz anything God commands He gives us the ability to do it ALL, amen?

Instead of being mad at people it helps to see it's something coming THRU them that's evil.

Saying "I can't help it" is just a sneaky way of not taking responsibility and you know it.

Why do we worry? Because we think we can figure out how to fix our problem instead of praying.

WOMEN SEEK APPROVAL THRU TRADITION

Women pressure daughters to follow tradition and that's where FGM and forced marriage comes in.

Remember: there's only ONE right link. Wait for him because everyone else will be rinky-dink.

KAREN KELLOCK 101

Speak against the government and you're a dissident labeled mentally insane, taken to the gulag.

In bubbles surrounded by sycophants then they crumble or remain good and taken out by evil.

Stop rehashing what you went thru and have gratitude God gave you victory in the feud.

She's a total breakaway from all decency. You can't criticize her cuz where would you start, really?

I realized suddenly I had problems in my soul from the early abuse being called bad or odd.

To be misjudged that way was so hurtful, so against the identity I had in God, it was just awful.

DEVELOPING A PRICKLY CRUST

So I developed a crust, spiny and prickly: the wounded-gathering-thorns syndrome.

Only after years of drinking at that crust did I break thru to my OWN reality, right-brained, best.

I was cast in that low role by a buncha idiots who were wealthy so thought they knew the way.

They were mean tyrants over me, very contradictory. You learn how to rule later best that way.

It was ruthless chaos--sending the check late or just in time and then making things right, aggravating.

They would jerk me around just cuz they could and make cruel officious remarks with impudence.

CONTROLLED BY LIBERAL HARRIDANS

It was verbal abuse by angry women telling me I'm no good and would never amount to anything.

And these angry harridans wanting to hurt me were in control of my finances for decades, see?

SO I KNOW what it's like to be controlled by liberal witch tyrants--I know the $$$ frustrations.

So illogical and cruel you wanna fight em but if you do you've had it so you become an addict.

I went thru all that for decades just so I could tell you these things: when women rule, they sting.

It's the JEZEBEL SPIRIT raising it's ugly head and I do mean ugly--inside and out eventually.

Feminists: Impertinence, insolence, cheek, audacity, brazenness, immodesty, shamelessness.

And now without limits, they sink to even lower depths of depravity in foodsex "mukbangs".

Talking about perverse sex while eating mountains of junk food in archetypal Dionysian madness.

Abused/misused you, abandoned/betrayed, ridiculed/mocked/rejected but God saved the day.

ANSWER COMES BEFORE THE PROBLEM

To brokenhearted after rejection: Jesus has already set you free, He has the solution for thee.

Coming out of the prison doors--which already have open doors--to see your destiny, and soar.

You've been saved but your mind's still a garbage pit like waking up in fits. Clear the mind, be LIT.

KAREN KELLOCK 101

I was saved but many of my thoughts were dark and lonely--I still hadn't learned to think rightly.

Once the lowly take control over you it's a teaching experience educating the future emperor.

Emotions a mess, can't abide people and triggered when Satan put thoughts in my head.

We can't stop Satan from putting thoughts in minds but we can jet em out/replace with kind.

CONTROLLING THOUGHTS

We can't stop Satan from putting thoughts in minds but we can jet em out knowing who's behind.

Don't go by your feelings cuz they don't tell the truth/they're fickle--go deeper, let God tell.

Since feelings are at war with each other you never know when flesh will show up/Satan's clever.

So you gotta go by what you know not by what you feel because usually that's from below.

You MUST walk by what you know not what you feel cuz that vacillates and Satans seeks to steal.

What do we know: We know that God is faithful and that he has a plan for you and your family.

I felt no confidence and my words had no power, I was totally lackluster and moods were sour.

All cuza what my sister said, are you kidding me? No, and it lasted decades, what a tragedy.

You're not timid and shy and fearful but a child of God--and children speak boldly as we know.

BE NOT AFRAID OF CHANGE

A confident woman is not afraid of change. That's because it's God behind her not a cage.

A confident woman in fact wants God to shake things up sometimes, not the same old/same old.

They won't try cuz they're so afraid of making mistakes but even so, God can change em.

And if I make a mistake it just doesn't matter that much cuz God can fix it--incredible, isn't it?

A confident woman is not double-minded, constantly making decisions then changing her mind.

They can be indecisive, impulsive or reckless or even worse, they'll get restless then start to bitch.

Be decisive: You need to know what you believe and stick with it--never by the polls, they're twits.

You need to KNOW what you are to do and lock onto it--like a big pit bull refusing to let it go.

GOD'S SOLUTIONS ARE ALWAYS SO CLEVER

You need to know what you believe about what God wants for your life and go for it despite strife.

The world is full of brokenhearted people whose broken personality can't function at their best.

Whenever God brings the solution it's something I never could have thought of it's so shrewd.

Worry does no good at all, never solving the problem but most likely increasing it's bad potential.

KAREN KELLOCK 101

Worry steals our peace and it means we're not trusting God to solve our problems, so cease.

What a relief it was to trade in worry for trust and prayer--always answered with clever flair.

Every time a bad thought arises I say "SATAN" and that trick is really extinguishing it fast.

Self-control is a **FRUIT** of the spirit and applies not only to behavior but more **WHAT WE THINK.**

Be strong, have self-control: never be a salivating or terrified slave of your thoughts or get **OLD.**

Your thoughts can make you old before your time from the constant adrenalin for the fight.

All day and night long being angry over something that happened 35 years ago, how inefficient.

That's what Satan wants: for you to be **WORN OUT** from memories getting you going, what a rut.

Not only did it exhaust me, it ran down my immunity til I was sick on top of a mental catastrophe.

CURE THE MIND THRU OLD MOVIES: MENTAL TRANSPORT

To cure the mind I had to switch to old movies for awhile, a mental transport filled with style.

Trump: The more they hate him the less they understand him--why/how he talks is not their thing.

The things they don't react to [seared conscience] he doubles-down on with acute intelligence.

All the lecturing I had to endure from liberals before I knew the truth—and they felt so superior too.

I wasn't nice enough, social enough {accommodating and compromising}, I wouldn't shut my mouth.

I always preferred solitude so would forget their social events and would get lectured for that.

Since churches changed they bored me silly. I want hellfire sin-repentance, hell-heaven preaching.

They acted like I didn't love God cuz I wouldn't go to their boring socials and potlucks.

I hated groups my whole life. I pick up on everything like strife. One/two people max I still feel alive.

At this point in time, it's YOUR time and will never be again, so hold your head up high and go on.

Contenders like Beto are sickly sweet, packaged and full of hype coming from soulless parasites.

Feeling separate from the pack creates shame which is an easy set up for addiction in so many.

DUNNING KRUGER IS IN EFFECT

My best advice is: accept no advice from anyone and I mean anyone unless specifically requested.

Remember, Dunning-Kruger is in effect: they all think you're dumb and that they know best.

It's INSULTING advice. There's a hidden message every time that you're not worth a dime.

Many artists were split into a million pieces but narcissistic enough to turn it into money.

I'm not the character I create and that is OK. Playing out another self is relieving and really pays.

KAREN KELLOCK 101

Your whole problem was inferior characters around you who misadvised and debased your morals too.

He allowed me to go thru all that to learn what people were like and I learned and never went back.

The superior man has empathy for his animals. That means: turn it all off and PUT THE MUSIC ON.

PREVALENT AGEISM

When they audaciously ask you your age dude, say "uh oh, you shouldn't have asked that, it's rude"

Cuz if you tell em your age they may reject you--objectify, we cry--and that we can't chance.

In an ageist society they objectify by age so by you revealing it you take that chance.

The superior man or woman can't allow that--why would they ask age anyway? For good? NOT

Caving into their question gives them a chance to reject you cuz prevalent ageism is TRUE.

Would they ask you your RACE? Don't think so, they'd be afraid to--but ageism is WORSE.

In a callous ageist [non-traditional] society, a number automatically discounts your worthiness.

If they rejected you cuz you're too old then don't take em back when they're out in the cold.

Hey, ageist idiot: I'll age and die and then YOU will be old, get it?

SAGACITY IS SICK OF THEIR PROJECTIONS

The guy asked me my age and I blocked him then wrote two pages on ageism, thank you friend.

You can so easily find a person's age on the internet, you don't have to do that/put em on the spot.
An older person--a sage--is so sick of their projections they know how to deal with em.

An older person--a sage--is so sick of their projections he knows how to deal with em.

Because their reactions have whole culture behind em you must react by escaping the scene.

I don't need your friggin' projections! I've HAD IT with all that, I am who I am you dam rats.

Listen up guys: If you ask a woman her age she'll automatically hate you--test it, it's true.

Because we know about ageism, how a woman panics at 30, and we think it's shitty.

Feign interest in an older person--well established--just to suck money out of the Mr. or Mrs.

They act like old age is a DIRTY thing, a laughable, silly thing soon to die out like ol' dinosaurs.

So of course we panic at 30, or even the thought of it, since it's obvious we become obsolete.

Ageism is the opposite to a traditional culture in which status increases with age/the mature.

RETIRE TO AVOID AGEISM

Traditionally the OLD held society together and UP and were granted first seats in the senate.

They disdain the gatekeepers--the key to their destiny but ignored by the nasty youthist culture.

KAREN KELLOCK 101

What does youth know? Generally nothing, esp. now as sensual sins are accepted and exploding.

Great actresses better with age retired early just to avoid the mean, cruel ageist comments.

Great actresses better with age retired early just to avoid the mean, cruel ageist comments.

We need Donald Trump to handle the homeless crisis cuz his track record shows he can do it.

The subconscious knew I had just finished 100 books and I slept for three days, flat out.

The seared conscience of the conformist masses vs. the hypersensitivity of poets, artists and empaths.

Good fences make good neighbors and the worst thing possible is to be unprotected out there.

We don't need walls? How stupid—you don't block home invaders with a fence working like magic?

We're having mass ICE raids now with major local pushback for those against the United States!

Since liberals are lawless they don't care they're "illegals" cuz laws themselves are ridiculous.

Tho' AOC's an idiot it doesn't make her less dangerous and if smart we won't forget that.

Only one excuse for a woman not to keep good house and that's if she's in poor health.

GREATEST VALUE: INDEPENDENCE

Greatest value is independence which only comes from small government or they're in your face.

The greatest gift of the Renaissance was human rights not bloody heathen sacrifice.

The bible says to avoid useless debate--that's what it is with critical leftists who think they're great.

Can't believe FOX is reporting on Biden or whomever and not HONG KONG's imminent slaughter.

The Hong Kong protestors are fighting for their lives cuz the ChiComs will take em to the gulags.

NEVER argue with a leftist cuz they're arrogant and that triggers frustration in God's Elect.

Since he can't debate with facts the leftist always distracts to your conflations or poor logic.

The reason they call each other crazy is there's TWO SEPARATE REALITIES: male and female.

I can't pinpoint the etiology of my neurosis without blaming the dead so RIP: I'll be good instead.

There's also a male vs. female intelligence and therefore also a male vs. female neuroses.

Mutual understanding of these differentials solve many arguments and make happy couples.

When a male starts to bash my IQ or worldview like so often before it's that conflict I abhor.

USELESS DEBATES WITH MENTAL MIDGETS

I don't need to get into a turgid nasty debate with a sophomoric male picking apart my "illogic".

City Decline: The richness of a city forces up land prices then middle class leaves for the suburbs.

KAREN KELLOCK 101

So not only are you arguing there's the added stress of him PUTTING DOWN your way of thinking.

I'm never gonna waste my energy like that again in an urge to "win"--useless, depleting fretting.

Besides, you knew he was wrong from the beginning so now just forget him and enjoy your evening.

I can't believe I live in comfort and safety after the prison of a small liberal town of the catty.

Small liberal towns: Catty backbiting, whispering, slandering, manipulating, lying, gossiping.

SECRET ALLIANCES AND TRIANGULATIONS

Liberal towns are feminist: every time a new girl arrives all the women display their fists.

You talk facts, he responds with amorphous abstracts and calls you crazy as an added hex.

You went thru this once you're crazy to do it again unless you wanna regress back as the dunce.

Have enough self-respect not to be picked apart by a Dunning-Kruger effect/him thinking he's great.

When I blocked the sophistic Pharisaic arguer I felt so much better and saw the male-female fetter.

Secret coalitions means everything's behind your back. Triangulation = suffocation in fact.

Anorexic system is marked by secret coalitions and this frustration keeps the system running.

THEY MISTREAT YOU, GOD PROMOTES YOU

One person mistreats you and then God promotes you--because He is the God of Justice too.

You thought evil against me but God meant it for good. Joseph to his brothers, Genesis 50: 20.

God used that cruel family situation to get Joseph into a place of helping the entire nation.

They boiled over with so much hatred, envy and anger they sold to slavers their own brother.

I recall being hated that much and I'm sure you do too--extremely dangerous and not for a few.

His family did all that awful stuff to him but God was with him and he ended up the king, Egyptian.

ALL things fit together for good for those who love God [for joyous faith this must be understood].

Don't let their hostility change who you are [which I did for years] and eventually it ends the war.

SMALL TOWN POLITIX

Before I gained necessary confidence and verbal alacrity to not be called crazy, it was a tragedy.

Cuz if you don't conform to their narrative you were the enemy and women would attack, really.

I was thrown into the mindgames of caring what the small townspeople thought, tied up in knots.

The more I let it bother my hypersensitive soul the more prickly I got thus making a bigger target.

Do not forget the basis of your nagging shame--it's from standing out from the pack today.

Shame has a biological basis to maintain the pack, the herd, the tribe so let it go--BYE-BYE

They're doing worse stuff but cuz they're accepted it's all ignored as normal, taken for granted.

NEVER COMPLAIN, NEVER EXPLAIN

Never complain, never explain. Mantra of the Royal Family for Hundreds of Years.

They make flowery unsubstantial speeches about saving the planet but then they jet out.

If they're not on board with it, if they're holding back a well deserved complement, forget it.

We traditional women don't need International Women's Day to be strong, we ARE strong.

Never complain, never explain and RARELY be heard speaking in public. Mantra of the Royal Family

WE MISS YOU HARRY

Prince Harry--what a puppet. Meghan's a leftist and he's so whipped he's going along with this.

Why you phony copying my stuff. And it's just the title, you don't have it filled out/ALL BLUFF.

Diana said Prince William was sensible and bright but Harry was NOT bright and easily influenced.

It's insulting what Harry's saying. "We're the ones who care", you stand for nothing--left wing.

The Mad Millennials in England apparently love hearing Prince Harry spew this stuff.

They literally don't know any better cuz they weren't taught character and what a disaster.

You give em something they just want MORE and have no compunction about asking for.

You've planted a huge seed and nothing happens but as time passes you're closer to blossoming.

The little jealous person will "pop off" in sting-shots about your age, looks or whatever.

The Squad appeals to Millennials so is proud of that but most of Americans hate their guts.

There's no competition with youth, remember that. We cower in a youthist society but it's all blab.

We really miss you Harry! Stop being a puppet of a feminist leftist--it's boring, peculiar and scary.

FORGIVE FEMINIST MOTHER TO MATURE

A boy cannot mature until he's forgiven his mother because inside he's so darn mad at her.

Jezebel planted evil seeds with major people so when I moved in I had MUCH to deal with.

Jezebel seems humble at first but give her an inch and she REARS UP AGAINST YOU like a curse.

They won't admit it but many men hate their mothers and wives cuz they're friggin' feminists!

It's disgusting how they go along with the narrative whatever it is to avoid female rejection.

Because they wanna be liked they don't have a mind of their own--even church ladies are like clones.

And this conformity makes them SO dangerous ya see cuz they're unreliable for you and me.

WAIT FOR DUST TO SETTLE

The dust has settled and I am left standing here. They're all dead or gone and I've got flair.

I will not go anywhere where they're gonna give me advice when I never asked em for it, forget it.

Jezebel will plant evil seeds with your neighbors. Suddenly they're hostile, avoidant or at war.

Jezebel could be your mother telling all your worst behaviors and evil deeds to perfect strangers.

Jezebel could be your sister who can't keep her trap shut for a minute and causes you messes.

Some people are destined to be famous but when immature they go the wrong way about it.

Biggest money makers on youtube are mukbangs: gluttony combined with small talk.

When Jezebel gets restless fever she'll get all her friends against you and bring em over.

ZEZEBEL IS A TALKER

They can't keep their pie holes shut and it's constant back and forth, chirping, primping, mimicking.

The worst part is when Jezebel gets with lawyers and paints her evil pictures--you are censured.

The worst part is when Jezebel's in control of the finances--you will soon seek independence.

KAREN KELLOCK 101

And they will beat your ass and get away with it. The cops and all departments are a feminist set up.

Females didn't used to be this way. They were tender, caring, neat and sweet little ladies.

An older harridan will KILL the new woman on the block. Ruthless sadists vs. Karen Kellock.

And no house is big enough for two women. I'm talking about sadistic competition too man.

Even the Queen's maids are cruel. Singing songs with lyrics about the old crone and shrew.

The maid reared up at me with cruel words of venom I could see in her eyes, I dismissed her fast.

Women are cruel to each other and can't be trusted, but what of their sons--hexed, raised by feminists.

Most dads aren't around, the boys are raised/take on the feminist view and act like women too.

Instead of calmly doing the manly thing--just doing it--they complain bitterly or displace blame.

Of course I'm not talking about ALL, not all. Those who break through become the best of y'all.

Women are taking over everywhere and the "future is female" they say. It's a terrible scare, ok?

WITH JUST A KEYBOARD AND ROCKS

With only a keyboard and rocks the SJWs tirelessly protect America from fake racism and sexism.

You aren't abnormal as they say, you're just different from other people so they'll see you that way.

KAREN KELLOCK 101

Let the past go--it was just your painful preparation for your new life a mature lady with a mansion.

Don't go back and pick it apart or analyze--it was terrible yes but that's why you'll now amaze.

The mere fact they could fit into the California fabric shows who they are so promptly forget it.

You can't drag the past into the future unless you want the future ruined for sure.

I don't want anyone around who constrains me thru his projections, it's aggravation/destruction.

He's socially hypnotized, I'm not so I have to deal with his constant criticisms or why nots.

THE LEFT LOVES THE CHICOMS

The ChiComs are using mass migration to subsume Hong Kongs identity and create disunity.

It's not teaching em "critical thinking" but insidious indoctrination and they get violent about em.

When you get into the circular part of the debate, bow out it's a liberal and it's third rate.

The liberals on TV will not answer the question, ever. No matter what the form, they filibuster.

Their argumentation is circuitous as they bring up non-issues/we're pressured by Dunning-Kruger.

Arguing with them brings you down to their level, stamping out fallacies and fighting the devil.

State the case but then you don't have to get down in the muddy trenches with arrogant creeps.

Worked all his life, at the top of his game at 70 then someone says "you're over the hill buddy".

Liberals never answer questions they circuitously hammer their crazy narrative like bumpkins.

HAVE BORDERS OR BE TAKEN OVER

What I learned in my life: If you don't have boundaries and borders you will be taken over.

Recap: If you're weak and not assertive you will be put thru the ringer by family justice warriors.

They started witchin' about my white privilege at age sixteen and guilt made my whole life change.

Why should you debate with a lower level? Just their viewpoint alone indicates they're the devil's.

Einstein/great minds just wanted to be alone but people would travel far to debate the throne.

It's circuitous and filled with non-issues--why would those great minds want that, I behoove?

Let your work stand on its own. Soon you won't be here to defend it anyway so separate now.

You already know they're wrong the mere fact they're disagreeing with you, so eschew.

Arguing with a liberal is like going down a rabbit hole--what about this, that, the other...

Thousands of troops over Hong Kong bridge and the protestors know what they're up against.

Going back is like swimming upstream thru muddy waters filled with dangers--don't go there.

KAREN KELLOCK 101

The mere fact they're not equally horrified by these things means arguing is useless and tiring.

"Global citizen" doesn't mean what it sounds like, just another euphemism for an awful thing.

GOING BACK IS SWIMMING UPSTREAM IN MUD

And I can already hear their arguments starting up, so what--ignore em completely, fence up.

It triggered a lot of "ego alien material"--weird crap from the collective unconscious of y'all.

It wasn't "me" it was the weird stuff coming thru me cuz I was weak with porous boundaries.

It was also the weird crap from the bad associations I had at the time--spirits gross and unrefined.

People who had no restraints--children in the self-control department, anything goes, dark, bent.

WATCH THE MERE CONTACT

With mere contact you think "anything can happen with these people", very bad instincts.

These people don't care about a thing. Dark or missing hearts, brazen, angrily left-wing.

Beta males must forgive their feminist mothers before evolving to alpha males or soldiers.

He doesn't realize he was mad at her since he introjected her feminist view-- "good boy".

That's his identity--a feminist male, a good boy--so he's able to misfire/transfer his mother anger.

KAREN KELLOCK 101

He can't help but hate her since feminism is illogical and the enforcer can be irascible as hell.

She changes her mind with the winds or talking to others or viciously adamant about whatever.

She's so socially-driven she changes her mind after talking to Katherine on petty doctrine.

Don't take on their attitudes on anything esp. meat because so much of this is virtue signaling.

Like everything else they do, it's all about how they appear in the eyes of others and life is skewed.

THE OTHER-DIRECTED ARE MENTALLY EFFECTED

They say obscene and cruel things to be part of the club. It's so embarrassing--please grow up!

Hah hah but that's also how we see who they are. They are lackluster losers, the non-stars.

The kids are totally dangerous. There's nothing they won't do and it's a badge of honor to kill you too.

I would never get involved with someone so other-directed again: completely out of grace/SIN.

They don't have an inner life/make socially-based decisions. it's about the others, get this.

Because they're conformists fools they are cruel. They lack empathy cuz it's mob-driven, see?

It's all about you're too prudish [not cutting them enough slack]: mean, old fashioned, snobbish.

All because you don't want girl and boy going into locked room in the house--utterly ridiculous!

KAREN KELLOCK 101

Let alone all the other filth mom and dad has to put up with, seen as "normal" and taken for granted.

If I were you I'd run it like an army barracks with exact routines punishable by lost goodies.

You must do this: As you dis-reward slackers and procrastinators then pick out/reward the best.

THEY SAID IT COULDN'T BE DONE

They all said it couldn't be done, whatever it was I was doing: working while avoiding phonies.

You work all your life to get their approval and when you [almost] finally get it it's irrelevant to you.

The loud bass and rap appeals to our baser, grosser emotions: self, affluence, jealousy, garishness.

I'd rather the music trigger tranquility, stability, peacefulness, security, creativity, God.

I love Martin Denny cuz he takes me back to beginning--at 12 he conjured up dreams for me.

I love cocktail music from the fifties--a different time altogether, the psychology of a better era.

Fifties music is like a magic mental transport to a healthier time and it works like a charm.

Remember, it's SHAME which results from misfitting the pack then this attaches itself to this or that.

Once you take the guns you have lawless gov, lawless criminals and all the rest of us unarmed slaves.

STOP being victimized by thoughts. Choose em better when they go by, or be a victim/NOT.

Sucking Spirit: Sucking up everything in its path out of obvious and obnoxious neediness! A turn off, I'll watch that.

Despite every stinking unfair thing that's happened day and night, God makes ALL things right.

If God's not in it it's not gonna work anyway and if He's in it there's no one who can stop it.

DOUBLE FOR YOUR TROUBLE

The reason I have so many things is God gave me double for the trouble I had with the rabble.

God makes it double: God gives us a twofold recompense for our former troubles. Isa 61: 7

Whenever bitter just mutter: I've got a double blessing on the way from God my Provider.

After men and family abused me for years God gave me a place of honor, there's no more tears.

It's a lot harder to keep praising God when NOT getting what you want but it maxes you out.

Tired of circular debates with worthless liberals. Third rate, would rather be alone that's all.

Of course the noxious events stand out in memory but what of the long respites God gave thee?

My eyes go out to the horizon for I know my source. When things become too much just look up.

It's not happening now but you feels you're in a war zone, all cuz you let thoughts in your home.

Devil knows just what thoughts to put in your mind. He knows your Achilles heel and He reminds.

KAREN KELLOCK 101

You gotta block bad thoughts like you would block a rabble of teenage invaders of your house because:

NARCISSISTS GO BY THEIR FEELINGS

Always recall that narcissists are troubled souls--underdeveloped like a child in all their roles.

He simply hasn't figured out yet that the whole world doesn't revolve around him/her, get it?

And even if he tries to correct it he goes too far the other way as a mamby-pamby sycophant.

To the extent the narcissist over-values himself he undervalues you, just a pawn to use.

Sociopaths are always cooking up a scheme while thinking: "none of these rules apply to me".

Rules and morality are irrelevant to the narcissist--it's whatever they **FEEL** in the moment.

Narcissist characteristics: no remorse or guilt. If you reward him thru forgiveness he just repeats it.

When you or I do wrong we agonize over it and soul-search. Sociopaths don't do this or feel worse.

They do/say whatever's expedient in the moment with zero accountability to you or whomever.

Narcissists are mask-wearing chameleons living to exploit so avoid em like plague/God will anoint.

The psychopath is a little different, he has **ZERO** conscience--do you know one by chance?

NARCISSISTS SEE PEOPLE AS TOOLS

Caring for no one but themselves they have no need for compassion, empathy or anything else.

People are only tools to be used so they are coldblooded in the way they engage too.

Because of all this they **MUST** be dominant and can have a bad temper when maintaining it.

They're so prone to bad temper maintaining dominance they can be very dangerous.

He/she has a reckless disregard for any kind of order or your border with no remorse whatsoever.

Since everything they do is for themselves they're grabby and out of grace with your stuff.

They operate on the fringes of society and are unable to hold a job since they can't be told.

Whether a dismissive, schemer or psychopath all three have one assumption: you are beneath them.

There is no "equality" or democracy with these three, you only exist to be exploited, sorry.

What you see is not reality with them. You're dealing with smoke and mirrors/good luck on what happens.

DRAWN TO BAD BOYS/WILD GIRLS

They have no regard for your well being, so stick with them and you'll be very harmed eventually.

Why you must give up on them: They can't stand correction and they can't see the dysfunction.

Are you drawn to the bad boy/wild girl mentality? Think hard before you ever commit to insanity.

KAREN KELLOCK 101

They are collapsars and destroyers not builders, constructors, creative source or expanders.

Satan is the counterfeiter--not the real, the bones, the guts, the bonafide or the real source.

Always before a collapse in civilization, people become demanding, dependent and needy.

These people fake their way thru life until they meet someone real who's invincible to their lies.

When the Act doesn't work they shift into gear but there comes a time when they gotta get clear.

I became real when I met a man invincible to my spiel and it was immediate, he's my husband too.

Symptoms endure and harden cuz they WORK and when they don't you either cure or die man.

Underneath I was terrified every moment of him, he was entirely unpredictable without any limits.

I had examples of his utter cruelty but due to weak boundaries stayed despite nightmares nightly.

HOLLYWOOD, BIG PHARMA, GLOBALISTS

In all cases across the world, take the guns and the crime rate explodes a hundred times over.

Cops want armed civilians. More than 90% support concealed carry, making their job easier man.

Since 1934 there are only TWO cases of machine guns used in a crime yet they're the problem?

Since Big Pharma finances the schools of course they say supplements are the same as food.

Hollywood portrays gun owners as dumb hicks or ragtag armies, not responsible patriots.

94% of mass public shootings in the US occur in gun-free zones, so please arm your homes.

Hollywood bias is everywhere misleading people about the importance of carrying guns as evil.

Socialism and Shariah law: a deadly combination to any society coming thru the democrat party.

FGM: One hour "procedure" recalled for life with horror while love is replaced by dismay/betrayal.

FGM [clit cutting] has a lifelong effect. You never recover from it you just learn to live with it.

BETRAYALS IN TRADITIONS

I was your sister, you meant everything to me--but then you replaced me in pure treachery.

I was a blank slate for their projections and couldn't fight back as I was spiraling down exhausted.

You terrorized and tormented me for years and now you come back because I'm a rich seer.

They tormented and terrorized by IMPOSING on me like Blanche in Streetcar named Desire, see?

Only a little lady trained to be quiet and compliant can know the horror of what this is like.

CUCKHOLDED BETA "MALE FEMINISTS"

Harry was ripe for the picking and Meghan Markle was a well-seasoned hunter I'm thinking.

With 9 million followers that's their constituency and they don't care about whether you like em, see?

Artists: When they're on stage they'll perform but when not they just wanna be left alone.

Go to Eastern Europe because France/Rome/London are more dangerous than Baghdad now.

You don't leave a man because men are emotionally brittle and they will suicide or just die.

The stupidest thing ever is a woman thinking she doesn't need the man or a man the woman.

HodgeTwin "Conservatives" say God made perverts so go along with it or you're a bigot.

The feminist just naturally thinks: How can I work this? How can I manipulate this connection?

TESTED AND TRIED THEN THE PRIZE

I'm thru with stuffing myself with info for awhile. Cuz the best is inside and filled with so much style!

God tested and tried them as He led them in the wilderness that He might do them good.

He tested and tried them FIRST before He then led them into the Land of Milk and Honey.

Torture, death, three days THEN the resurrection. In all areas it's the exact same pattern, amen.

My only problem is reliving the torture when brings mental closure against all new adventures.

It takes TIME to remember/go thru all this stuff--too much of the pie, for success nothing left.

And the anger and resentment it congers up--all for something that's gone forever: STOP.

It's not that you have bad relationship techniques but that you've been around a buncha lower creeps.

Stop wasting your breath on me. I've seen God, I know God, and I know what He can do, ok?

Never argue with a leftist empiricist demanding proof when these "intellectuals" remains so stupid.

Tho' her evil was palpable and housekeeping terrible she was voted "most helpful" by the rabble.

AVOID ALL EVIL HELPERS

Avoid all evil helpers. To do this you must realize your moral independence from these losers.

The evil helper is just a way in the door. Wicked men always want in to bring chaos, bedlam, rancor.

He did not trust Himself to His disciples for He knew human nature.

We shouldn't give trust to people that belongs only to God, for human nature is erratic and odd.

A mature person has no unrealistic expectations that people will never hurt us. Joyce Meyer

You may feel that your whole life is over but little do you know, it may be just the beginning.

God intends us to have incredible lives but not if remaining wounded in backstabbing strife.

In this modern society practically everybody is a wounded soul until they collapse when old.

Joseph's brothers hated him/sold him into slavery and he went to prison but God was with him.

The more victimized by people the more you'll find favor by everyone after repenting of all evil.

PEOPLE ARE THE ENVIRONMENT

Depending on others or bunking up is a terrible prison of mal-adaptations to the punk.

Who we are around/who we adapt to IS our environment and in psychology it's crucial.

So you DON'T let anyone in your house cuz you don't wanna adapt to them-- keep your house clean.

The importance of environment is lost to most--but it rewires our brains and turns em to toast.

Just by letting ONE bad guest in he ruins the whole household. I can attest to this, I know.

The idea of people bringing others to your home unvetted by you is so immature and high school.

People in the environment to whom we adapt: They don't have to say anything, it's mental crap.

Their officious questions that take you back or yank your chain with unnecessary flack.

SHOCKING INSIGHT: HERD IS POWER

It's a shocking insight to see the herd for what it is--it's bigger than you are when having influence.

I have no memories of 20 years solitude, only noxious recalls from people problems/feuds.

My anxieties never left until alone, then it was **BLAST OFF** to mental discoveries and destiny/my throne.

People coming and going like grand central station is simply disgusting--think of the pets scaring.

Don't let men into your home alone. It doesn't look right and it isn't right, you should be chaperoned.

That class from high school in '85 were entitled creeps who were debauched and obscene.

MORE VICTIMIZED, MORE FAVOR LATER

Why do I get double for my trouble after being victimized by people? Cuz God is on my side.

If God is on my side, whom shall I fear? He won't keep you from going thru it but still He's near.

When souls are wounded from abuse, unjust treatment or rejection the result is guilt/shame.

Choose today to not live wounded but to live the life Christ died for you to have, grounded.

Ask God to rework each unfair event to your benefit, and to help others who are wounded with it.

PIE. You're not going forward in God's plan if you hate someone from the past doing you wrong.

No matter what happens/did happen a trusted God will turn it to good, a truth I stake my life on.

It makes us a better person. If we don't get anything else outa the tragedy it must be compassion.

The best way to get a boatload of compassion is to go thru this horrible painful stuff yourself.

Don't fall victim into the trap of equality when it's **NOT EQUAL** and never will be for ya'll.

Don't fall victim to the demon of equality in the marriage like a man crying unembarrassed.

Are you an emotional guy or a stable stoic? Don't react emotionally and this is being grown up.

The stable stoic does not deny his emotions but delays them: he is steadfast, solid and firm.

JESUS HAS THE SOLUTION BEFORE THE PROBLEM

Jesus has already set free the brokenhearted person. That's the good news, we can change it.

I would vacillate between being in control to being controlled and that's not our divine role.

He sent him to bind up and heal the brokenhearted. Wow, that was me but now I have my Father.

What a revelation: I didn't have to be trapped in my past or by slander by those who miscast.

An ornament of beauty for ashes: that's how God does things, in the end it's all balancing.

Twofold recompense for prior troubles: **PAYBACK IS BIBLICAL.**

Double blessings for former trouble: Nothing could be more biblical, good news for y'all.

Beauty for ashes, double for your trouble--why? Because I the Lord am a God of Justice.

God of Justice means: He makes everything that is wrong, right.

Bible definition of "restoration": To receive back more than you lost--what a revelation.

Exploding in popularity: Gluttony mukbangs with small talk combined with edgy sex talk.
GUTS FULL OF FIBER

With a daily fasting regimen of 22 hours your dietary selections are healthier each day and energizin'.

High-fat means far less bulk for equal satiety.

Your gut is destroyed by all the fiber and the anti-nutrients in the plants (don't wanna be eaten).

Vegans get energy from the constant sugar rush combined with adrenalin from plant toxins.

Typically vegans add tons of spice to their food cuz it tastes like crap otherwise: how cool.

Fruit smoothies, pizza or bacon: Counterintuitively, these are great for painless digestion I reckon.

The leftist "intelligent" women are cheap slaves approving of anything society approves of.

Tho' it's minus 15 nutrients in meat, the vegans love "fake meat" while deficiencies are depleted.

Kale is one of the most toxic things we could eat but the new age says it's the BEST thing.

SHAME is an identifier of bulimics and it's also from being separated from the pack or systems.

Vegans so crave meat that those fake meat burgers actually taste like meat to them at first.

As a vegan I knew there was something wrong when I got into crying jabs all day and night long.

DREAMING OF POT ROAST AND GRAVY

KAREN KELLOCK 101

I knew there was something wrong when I dreamed of pot roasts and gravy for which I longed.

After all that fruit and protein deprivation I longed for fatty, salty, meaty and not just dairy.

When you dream of pot roasts and gravy you know you're protein-depleted for this is the warning.

Fish, eggs or dairy may not help you that much. May have to go full meat not mere sandwich.

I don't like it any more than you do but feel I must FORCE feed meat at first, knowing the cure.

I've bought kitchen meat appurtenances but nothing's worked, it just goes into storage.

Now I'm buying a rotisserie hoping that'll interest me--can't I have my nutbutters/smoothies?

The psychological block against eating meat is very difficult to overcome/looks like anorexia to some.

For some reason fish is easier but it doesn't improve health that much, tho' a little some swore.

For some reason fish is easier but it doesn't improve health that much tho' it's tasty I'll say that.

MEAT-AVERSION: IS IT BIBLICAL?

Biblical: It may be this meat-aversion is spiritual and you'll never be able to eat it, that's all.

It's nearly impossible to reach a vegan before they deplete their stores. Then, who knows.

I'd love to rest on my nutbutters and smoothies but I know there's only one way: red meat.

KAREN KELLOCK 101

But how to overcome meat-aversion? I tried drying it but gave it to the dogs, now a rotisserie may work said God.
How to overcome meat-aversion? Tried drying it but gave it to dogs, now a rotisserie may work said God.

I'm just not interested in eating this, the one thing that totally cures, and I realize the split.

VEGANISM: MENTAL ILLNESS BLOCKS CURE?

Veganism produces mental illness and meat-aversion is the symptom blocking the cure.

It's definitely a sign of anorexia having to force yourself to eat meat or are we above it?

Or is this the body going into a fasting space because you're a saint?

All report INSTANT energy reviving their body with their first steak after the vegan tragedy.

I feel so great on nutbutters and smoothies but they say I gotta eat the meat--what is reality?

But there's things like extreme autoimmunity and esophagal pain preventing food after 9 am.

INSTANT ENERGY WITH FIRST STEAK?

So it's no small thing--will meat eating be the solution to this acid reflux pain?

Jordan Peterson said he was sick ALL the time before going carnivore then instantly well.

They say you cure leaky gut with greens but that's false due to lectins, oxalates and goitrogens.

What's left? Fruit and meat. The fruit I can do but the meat is such a chore, I'm so averse.

SRI's (antidepressants/antipsychotics) allow the lower brain to take over and we've had it.

Smoothies are the only way some can eat. It's so easy with a blender and it's nutrition-replete.

STOP PUTTING DOWN SMOOTHIES

Stop putting down smoothies. It is the only way cancer patients can eat in the last stages.

Stop putting down smoothies. It's the only way I can digest without pain and I sleep with ease.

Veganism brings depletion then meat-aversion, blocking the only cure for fatigue/exhaustion.

Meat-aversion: Keep saying I'll eat it convinced it's the only way but still just can't do it.

The bible does define two diet groups: meat eaters and meat abstainers so maybe that's it?

I love the cows walking by my house and we visit. When I think about their future I just can't do it.

I loved meat as a child but as you know we change with age--I'm an entirely different person/sage.

These people are dense/callous about a lot of things so of course they'd be to animals, ya think?

FIFTIES EATING IS BEST LOOKING

I knew a man in 70s with meat aversion. He glowed like a light living on bakery goods/sweet buns.

I noticed vegans would look great at first but with depletion would gradually fade like a curse.

I noticed moderate meat eaters of the American diet in the 1950's looked the best, like movie stars.

I noticed many vegans looked puffy if over-reliant on starches to satiate and prevent being hungry.

I noticed people living on fast food once a day then staying thin and being efficient, ok?

I noticed the skinny having HUGE daily breakfasts of it all but nothing more/not a morsel till tomorrow.

Moral of the story is: no one can tell you how to eat. It took me a lifetime to learn how I was unique.

I'm see the steak and it means nothing, it has no logic. I blend my food, it works like magic.

Tho' I'm in sweet-succulent mode, tomorrow I could go for fatty-salty meat mode, who knows.

I was a meat-eating child but as you know time ages us/changes us and it's a mental thing as well.

Mornings are associated with tuna, catnip and brushing--you should hear my 2 cats yelling.

I could eat pizza every day for my one meal: delicious, soothing, comforting, very digestible.

Maybe pizza is as close as I can come to animal fat and protein and besides it's my adaptive history.

EAT WHAT YOU WANT BUT FAST THEN CHOOSE UP

If you eat once daily [OMAD] there's no need for any diet. You may eat what you want, even fry it.

Forget the greenhouse--no anti-nutrients--and just buy freezers and stuff em with bacon/pizzas.

No lowcarb/ highcarb restrictions. Diets are mental constructions but the body's above em.

Either we starve to death or we die of toxic foods. Chinese food poisoning survivor

While fasting, mine the gems from the past. With your lucid recall this time is having a blast.

We are two offices side by side and no one constrains anyone and life is really fun.

If you work all your life and crest at 70 and they say you're over the hill then tell em to go to hell.

REVERSAL DIETING OF PALEO FOODS

At this point it's just smoothie meal replacements and grapes. I lost interest in pizza for a few days.

Haven't fixed bacon in two weeks. That today would be good to replenish protein stores and it's delicious, see.

I wonder if it's a new approach to fruitarianism: not as an ideology but cuz it's all you can eat?

Fruits and nutbutters: whew. After enduring so much I can't take the slaughterhouse too.

I just can't and I don't want to. My subconscious and body rebels at the mere thought of meat too.

I don't feel God will punish one like me with poor health cuz we can't eat that carnivore stuff.

When I was fruitarian before I dreamed of meat galore but now it's different, I'm really here.

For the chemically sensitive a toxic room is like being hit by a sledgehammer, a real bummer.

KAREN KELLOCK 101

Prince was vegan and he looked great in his fifties--like a teen--but have fish/pizza on weekends.

MEAT-ONLY FOR IMMUNE HEALING?

MYTHS dispelled: Don't drink water it washes away the minerals and don't eat toxic vegetables.

The abrupt switch to meat comes on the heels of my last sickening reaction-- I now concede/agree.

I'm sold on the idea that meat-only will heal this autoimmune disease automatically/instantly.

Lived on avocados for years--now they make me sick with latex allergy, how very peculiar.

All the vegan foods I thought were so healthy like avo, which made the whole thing palatable.

Worthless plants and grains basically, when all you need is in the meat and I have agreed to this.

It's so difficult to eat meat after the vegan brainwash, you must force yourself then it's simple as.

I had to spice up vegan concoctions to make em delicious and even then they were ridiculous.

We're going to go get the meat now, I'm consigned. Now matter what I'm finally going to be fine.

New life goes from useless plant "nutrients" to recovery from autoimmunity with best of science.

Jordan Peterson was sick ALL the time and was INSTANTLY healed with meat, what a sure sign.

We've always known protein is essential for the immune system yet it took me so long.

Reacting to everything, instant sickness. Getting strong again with meat, more impervious.

We'll fix a roast today for the giant experiment. I'll keep you updated before I end this section.

THE ROAST EXPERIMENT/JUST CAN'T DO IT

If this works I'll be celebrating for weeks. As much as I love animals it's health I must first seek.

I'm still resigned to the meat but still can't eat it. Just not interested but God will direct/assist.

The suffering of yesterday was avocado [latex] allergy not from any meat-deficiency.

We'll go get the roast today and I'll assemble the spices for the dry rub, and think about it.

After I'm over the hump and broken into my meat-aversion from veganism, it'll all open up.

They say ovo, lacto or rasta-vegetarianism won't work to erase all deficiencies, am I cursed?

Am I going against my true nature by force-feeding meat or masking it with so many spices, replete?

I have met hardly any who has this much trouble, fear and doubt eating meat, it seems genetic.

It's like my whole soul mind shrinks from it, I think back to the slaughter and can't deal with it.

I don't know what else to say. I'm split. Mentally I need the meat, spiritually I recoil like a stink.

TROPICAL DIET: FRUIT, COCONUT, PORK: "FRUGI-CARNIVORES"

KAREN KELLOCK 101

The first time around I wanted to eat meat but didn't. This time, I just can't and don't really want it.

One answer is lacto-fruitarianism, fruit and cheese. No veggies cuz they're toxic like nightshades.

Pizza thrice a week, fish thrice, bacon twice--that's enough protein for a 100 pounder I guess.

A little sugar makes the medicine go down--do fruit smoothies make the medicinal effects go down?

I'm beef-averse but can eat bacon so pork chops would be as healing as the beef I reckon'

How about a tropical diet of fruit, coconut and pork? I don't need to go lowcarb, I'm thin and sharp.

Hmmm: Pork has always been America's breakfast meat and mom fixed it thrice a week.

The pork made me sick all day. Guess it's back to fruit and cheese--getting protein that way.

This era shows GREEN BLOAT: from fiber, anti-nutrients and the toxins in plants like oxalates.

I felt so incredibly good after a cheese quesadilla with triple cheese tho' it breaks all the rules, see?

BORN TO BE A MEAT-ABSTAINER

Veganism produces mental illness that protects itself from curative change thru meat-aversion. True?

Is orthorexia a subset of anorexia, or is it a mature scientist seeking truth so I can tell ya'?

I've stopped trying to eat meat. It feels good to give up and just enjoy fruit smoothies or cheese.

Bought numerous kitchen appliances for meat so I'd eat it but they all went into the basement.

I could eat bacon but the caramelization brought dark spots and acid reflux all day: pain again!

There's something dark about it. Compare beautiful succulent sweet fruit with slaughterhouse.

People given to clarity [psychic, deja vu, clairvoyant] really can't take it as their mind "goes back".

I just have to believe God made some of us for fasting, certain diets and even celibacy.

HEARTBURN FROM NON-FRUITS

A pastor friend said "If God told you to eat fruit then if you don't you'll suffer, acute": yeah, heartburn!

Everything but produce creates acid and green veggies are poison so fruit's all that's left.

Fruit: NO PAIN all day and night, good sleep. Non-Fruit: acid, pain, heartburn, insomnia, weep.

Tried to be fruitarian for decades but would always slip. Now, it's all i can eat/the rest God forbids?

Gonna die eventually anyway so I think, why eat it?

My God it is horrifying and saddening compared to a fruit tree. Come on people, can't you see?

I'm not saying it's wrong to eat meat, enjoy your meat! Just saying there's two kinds of peeps.

I'm not into astrology but have read Pisces wrinkle easily unless fruitarian and then, none.

Perhaps the more exalted or spiritual signs end up on simple fare: God's fruits or a little cheese.

Even nuts are goitrogens, I suppose the nutbutters too--but hunger's quieted by a spoon.

Can't go to a "doctor" who'll tell me to eat greens. That leaves no one save those for the meat.

The modern fruitarians {raw till 4} stuff too much starch. Return to Ehretism and skip lunch.

MODERN FRUITARIANS ARE GLUTTONS

The Father Fruitarian was Ehret who said FRUGAL fruit meals and forget other foods instead.

NOT eating truckloads of fruit {gluttarianism} and spuds and salads are ONLY a transition! Ehret

But the modern fruitarians are TOTAL GLUTTONS and increasingly it's about starch substitutions.

STARCH is no solution: Potatoes are nightshades and all grains [lectins] cause ugly leaky gut.

Alex Jones' new protein bars are FILLED WITH SOY! After all his lecturing us on soyboys, ole!

Never get protein from "protein bars" filled with soy cuz it's a scam and dangerous for girls/boys.

Gonna stop worrying about this, it takes too much time. Trust my instincts and go back to rhyme.

LACTO-FRUITARIANISM: FRUIT AND CHEESE

The fruit smoothie--cheesy quesadilla--fast 22 hours plan is working out spectacularly man.

I don't think I'm just controlling symptoms by intermittent fasting, it's a time of HEALING.

KAREN KELLOCK 101

Meat is no longer in my perception, it is not what I choose except in force-feeding and I refuse.

I don't want it, I can't bare it and I would seriously be crossing a line to eat it and would pay for it.

I can eat the cheese--ok fine, it gets the job done in the a.m. and gives me animal fat/protein.

That's after a fruit smoothie, yah I carb-up in the morning and I find it enlivening/refreshing.

The **ONE** flour tortilla is a delivery system for the fat, that's less crust than a pizza and convenient.

NOT GONNA FORCE FEED THE MEAT

I'm not gonna force-feed it. If I die cuz I didn't eat the meat I'd be surprised like God's not in it.

I love the fruit and can eat the cheese and a little nutbutter too if you please but no meat.

I'm meant to be a meat-abstainer, God designed it and it's His highest plan for me to be richer.

Psychic powers go up so much with fruit, fat and fasting that you sequester cuz it's scary.

But not by eating truckloads of fruit and starchy substitutions, that's not how you get this.

All vegans think about is food cuz they're starving for animal fat. Eat some cheese and that is that.

Smoothie, quesadilla with triple cheese, buenelo smothered in butter and cinnamon.

I can take **ONE** digestive burn a day but the rest of my energy I want to go towards healing, ok?

Forget the buenelo smothered in butter and cinnamon. It was too much so today I'm fastin'

Starch combined with fat gets stuck but it's just a signal to fast the next day/not bulk up.

Everything but fruit causes acid or oxalates--who want's this? I'm done with heartburn, hellish.

I'm finding out how little I need to sustain with fruit/high-fat with some carb. Found lowcarb tortillas, flour!

Fruit smoothie, cheese quesadilla or buenelo smothered in butter and cinnamon, fast 22 hours.

THE PROBLEM IS ACID: ERHET

If the problem is ACID as in "heartburn" the only solution is non-acid foods: FRUITS/no vegs.

Everything but fruits and vegetables goes acid and creates mucus, the basis of all disease. Ehret

But no acid fruits--they are murder day/night on the immuno-suppressed with pained esophagus.

A solution is to put strawberries or pineapple {acids] with celery, cucumber, coconut in blender.

Don't put down smoothies, the blender is a modern invention keeping many of us alive I'll betcha.

Ended breakfast yesterday with some rocky road ice cream. No reaction and woke up the bloodstream.

I'm not gonna be a dam dieter ever again. I eat what I want cuz the time is running out and I'm thin.

These lowcarb flour tortillas are just the delivery system for high fat cheese/butter breakfast.

KAREN KELLOCK 101

I eat this just to get the job done, so I can work all day without fatigue or hunger and have fun.

ICE CREAM CHEMICAL DESTRUCTION

Ice cream tastes like dairy heaven but it's frozen chemicals, soy, gum, corn syrup and other leaven.

You criticize my cheese but it's 100% better than all those chemicals in cans, bags or frozen TVs.

I said: don't bring home any more ice cream cuz it's not what it seems, so delicious but all chems.

Rocky road ice cream was so delicious I ate the whole thing but later hell to pay/acid reflux pain.

Their flavor testers make it so delicious you tend to over-eat it and that's obesity in a nugget.

Lights go off in your head with ice cream making you think you need it and I've even said that.

The delicious addictive ice cream later makes your joints hurt: body pain, first reaction to allergy.

Don't lie down after ice cream cuz you'll pass out from this shit and then choke in your sleep.

Tasters take your delicious ice cream and shove it, I can hardly move/it's chemical soup and I've had it.

Ice cream seems like dairy heaven--fatty, sweet, comforting--but it's chemical destruction honey.

DIETARY SEEKING, WILL IT EVER END?

The Ghandi diet is fruit, milk and nuts--so why not fruit smoothies, cheese [lacto] and nut butters?

KAREN KELLOCK 101

The pork made me sick all day. Guess it's back to fruit and cheese--getting protein that way.

Yes the vegans tend to load up on nut butters and yes it's cuz they want the fat but is it bad?

Veganism creates a mental illness that protects itself from curative change by meat-aversion.

Is it mental illness or spiritual wellness that prevents a person from eating meat? That's the question.

Every one of the 100 books has a different diet in it cuz I'm a curious dietary seeker darnit.

Why diet I'm gonna die anyway so I'll just enjoy it and luxuriate in the lovely night, morning and day.

The trick to losing weight is to eat HIGH calorie, not low calorie--packed with fat then fast all day.

Delicious refreshing ice cream: High-fat and high-calorie, you want that so you can then fast.

Never thought I'd say it but it's ice cream for my esophagus and I feel energized/fascinated.

Ice cream's filled with FAT and CALORIES--just what a body needs before a 1-2 day fast, please.

The ice-cream (high-fat, high-calorie) was so filling I didn't eat for 36 hours and lost weight, see?

SECRET TO LONGEVITY: AVOID PEOPLE

Age 109 woman says the secret is to avoid people--I so agree especially in this generation of evil.

Society is a Dionysian festival: Eating mountains of food while talking about sex, unbelievable.

KAREN KELLOCK 101

The eccentrics--the loners, isolates, mystics--live longer and are far healthier than conformists.

With people around it's one interruption after another, in solitude it's just you--and so clever!

Caution: If they care what people think and don't have their own thoughts they'll take you out.

While on a Sunday afternoon fast I think of all the previous silent Sunday afts throughout my past/ETERNITY.

I'm beginning to see the good life just ahead. Been giving things away, expensive but irrelevant.

The books are done, published and made available. That's your seed you know, so just party until.

The books are completely done and I've never felt such a feeling of completion and satisfaction.

Frankly I don't give a dam is my attitude now cuz the time is late and I've arrived/at my top.

I'm watcha call a prolific writer now. After writing the draft a thousand times it's automatic, pow.

With each moment I'm getting closer to my harvest and I bless another day of waiting in earnest.

I think it's time you leave it ALL behind cuz the time is late and you've gotta destiny so sublime!

STICKY FINGER HOUSEKEEPERS

They see something, they want it, it's theirs, that's it.

A housekeeper should be silent, unobtrusive, humble, thorough and never ask to borrow.

KAREN KELLOCK 101

A housekeeper shouldn't be checking out your things and then coveting and taking them.

A houeskeeper is the one person who's around all your stuff--keep an eye out for that sucking spirit.

For due to the prevalent communist spirit they will TAKE it whether they need it or not/trip you up.

They don't need it they just don't want you to have it cuz the communist spirit has made us mad.

I seek solitude when the maid comes but it's not real smart cuz she's free to give into temptations.

It's not the money I'm just sick of finding stuff missing so our home is closed to those helping.

THE CREATIVE ACT AND COMPLETION

He put eternity in my heart and sent me to earth with a purpose and a great desire to be of service.

Tapping into eternity in your heart lines you up with what your purpose is, so that's where you start.

It's not about me. I present to you this great and marvelous work and wonder for the elites.

It was my whole life and now I've given birth after decades of fertile anarchy and I feel great.

Fertile anarchy driving me crazy and underground games and it's all invisible until the end, aye.

CREATIVE ACT IS ALL PLANNED PLUS LINK

The Creative Act's all planned down to the greatest detail and the link always appears without fail.

KAREN KELLOCK 101

The underground fertile anarchy was a billion details in disorder, it was up to me to complete the jigsaw.

It may have appeared crazy at times--indeed, a lunatic and I'm grateful not to be locked up.

When defending myself in society I couldn't sort it out so I sought solitude and launched off.

I always saw a ghost--an adumbration--of the formula and I'd lock it into place in different eras.

Every theory has a formula and when I locked that into place--obstruction/elimination--I knew I aced.

In those middle years in desert wilderness I suffered from the officious but it made me a poetess.

I explored the DEPTH of my emotions which were as deep as the oceans to write about syndromes.

It hurt so much, I'd think "How deep can I feel?" and it was so maudlin on my tearstained pillow.

Ok now that I felt all that and went that deep, I can write about it. Again, God put me through it.

Just cuz someone hurts me, I don't have a right to RUIN their reputation but women do that son.

SHAME IS THE RESULT OF TWO THINGS

Joseph was cruelly treated by his brothers who hated him and sold him into slavery.

Shame is the result of two things: either you were ostracized or you were a filthy sinner.

You're a slave and willing receptacle to all their worst and meanest projections and you accept it?

Prayer: Praise should outweigh petition. Thank Him first THEN ask Him about the latest problem.

MENTAL TYRANNY

If you go along with tyranny you become weak but if you RESIST it you become strong. END END after prayer

Stress layered upon stress until it became a raging mental illness and she really looked it.

Much of it comes down to: Trust God and do good, sewing seed for the harvest we need.

There's always someone around who resents your blessings. Careful they don't take em. END

You shoved your shit onto me as if you were white as snow and not a sinner but I'm the winner.

The first half of life I was too busy defending myself to ever get into the moment or really excel.

I don't like social events--they're either boring, poisonous or hurtful and I've had enough of em.

There's always someone around who resents your blessings. Careful they don't take em.

You bring government in and it always centralizes it and jacks up prices. Free market: competitive.

I long to divorce from the Creative Act as well as the news bringing the blues, I want a mind cruise.

RETIRE TO THE RIGHT BRAIN

No more left-brain political videos, I wanna be a kid again. Totally right-brained from now on.

KAREN KELLOCK 101

I wanna be an artist like I was at 18 or a salsa trumpeter at 20--more of what I was originally.

I'm sick of the polemics which are endless and there will be no more debates I just wanna Ace.

Every single man I held onto to protect me ended up destroying me and I lost my true instincts.

I wouldn't want to be young again, always fighting off the bullies, the interlopers or the frenemies.

God wants us to have a fresh start. But they don't want us to have this so they muddy our aura.

I have the biggest achievement of my entire lifetime: a wall and a locked gate, raising my fate.

Well actually it's just still a fence but the wall is coming soon, kicking life up to the moon.

Of all actions just dreaming or looking out the window is most profitable.

I want attention, I wanna be read, I wanna be heard and have influence, what's wrong with that.

It's hard to have hubris--excessive pride and arrogance--when you anticipate death.

I read a book--such folderol! 90% of print is dross, its not necessary at all, a lot of words but nil.

A million things didn't work but ONE of em DID and that's your new life if the dreary past your forbid.

GOD IS ETERNITY NOT THE TEMPORARY

Years went on and things weren't improving but the eternal is invisible and what we see is temporary.

KAREN KELLOCK 101

The things we see are subject to change so trust not your senses but realize what God's power is.

Where you are is not permanent--lonely, addicted, struggling--so get ready cuz God said it.

Don't get discouraged by what you see cuz you don't know what God's doing behind the scenes.

If a caterpillar who can't fly suddenly becomes a butterfly God can do the same for you and I.

Don't look at past or present circumstances, keep eyes on the invisible knowing God's behind it.

Not just "get ahead" but supernatural opportunities and increase--that's God when you're led.

God will **CATAPULT** you into a new dimension and favor so get ready for your glorious future.

Once you pass the marker it's all acceleration with things happening sooner than you thought before.

You've experienced this before: a **SUDDEN** change. This is how it will happen so prepare to engage.

Forget creeps who imposed on you, detained and distracted for now your success is decided.

Stop fighting the past--those imposters are gone forever and you're free at last/will have a blast.

I have everything ready because I know things will change suddenly as God tells me every day.

You can't write 100 shocking books about how we've been forsook and nothing happens/bad luck.

GOD ISN'T A CLOUD WITHOUT RAIN

KAREN KELLOCK 101

He isn't the God of clouds without rain, what He started in me He will finish and I will gain.

I am Your servant, ask me anything and I will. Thanks for Your many blessings and words which thrill.

What happens to these books is all up to Him. I've given birth and will just wait with my friends.

No more dread over these books, it's up to Him—God is my Champion and He decides outcomes!

Superior Man knows he flies high above the masses so it's just a matter of managing the asses.

Sage said "people aren't important--stop worshipping them" and right then I looked up to Him.

It's ALL up to God--He decides everything and it's all planned so stop worrying man and just be awed.

Why do I fear more that I know God, than when I was a pagan? No more seared conscience I reckon.

WHY FEAR IF YOU'RE WITH GOD?

Why do I fear more knowing God than when I was a pagan? No more seared conscience I reckon.

God sets the date for your total financial success so please Him/forget promotions to the masses.

You weren't interested in me, just the peanut gallery of idiots comprising your fan base, see?

You can tell em all these things and they'll agree so you're much too satisfied to be interested in me.

Sage said "people aren't important--stop worshipping them" and right then I looked up to Him.

KAREN KELLOCK 101

Since the sixties we've been worshipping people and dismissing God and this brings His deadly rod.

What you did to me was horrible but I forgive you Joe Devil cuz God said I am supposed to.

The benefits of forgiveness is hard science: forgiving the ass frees you to high finance.

LUCRATIVE HUNCH OR HATE THEIR GUTS?

You'll never get that lucrative final hunch until you give up the mental clutter of hating their guts.

I've done my work, I'm done. Now we come to the most important part, the WAIT...then the fun.

With every book I wrote the dread came afterwards. Not gonna happen this time as I wait for my Lord.

Will you like it? Will they like it? Not gonna give into the spin or fan base panic, God is the magic.

I'm gonna work out in the yard and till the soil while I wait for God's reward for this, my lifelong toil.

I believe most are held down by past or present people and only get ahead by eliminating evil.

Men are held down by sex-dealing women who want men to worship them--it's the Jezebel spirit man.

Men are sex addicts, women are sex-dealers: What a sick system this is--get clear and be pure.

ESCAPE SYSTEM CRUTCHES

Escape these systems which are crutches that ruined ya. Independence is exhilarating, yah!

KAREN KELLOCK 101

You work 30 years but suddenly you're promoted. What happened? You got your wings as a poet.

It's too cruel, don't go back. Recall it's not people but principalities we're fighting/demons are a fact.

The progeny of gossiping tail bearers will surely suffer from calumnious sins of their ancestors.

God doesn't play around when it comes to stirring up trouble. A bolt of lightening and they're goners.

The house was paid off instantly when I got my wings, it's the hand of God and it's SUDDENLY.

The caterpillar becomes a butterfly suddenly. Before he was ordinary but is now beautiful to me.

Suddenly you have wings, SUDDENLY you're thrust ahead, suddenly all want to invest, be led.

SUDDENLY things exploded. I didn't just go to a new level but a new dimension as things accelerated.

It's all in the works planned before your birth: an exact time table which thru sin we shirk.

That's all I gotta say: Just continue to wait, knowing that's the whole thing not just the starting gate.

They're so dumbed you must refuse to explain and let em see it intuitively not just yank your chain.

FULFILL DESTINY OR MISS IT ENTIRELY

You may fulfill this destiny or through sin miss it all entirely and end up in the gutter or dead, see?

You'll never be a winner if a filthy sinner and if you get good breaks you'll just ruin it in the future.

My whole life i've seen God punish sinners/foes and reward the repentant--100% there's a sentence.

God designed my Creative Act, I was the co-creator by clicking in the jigsaw puzzle, that's a fact.

He predesigned it all before my birth--what a great and marvelous destiny opened after the curse.

Your idea of flying and God's are different. Wait until you get your wings and you'll be elated/affluent.

It's not a matter of how to get to success but how you handle it when you get there, BLESSED.

You haven't seen, heard nor imagined what God has in store--He's gonna open giant, lavish doors!

God Bless,

KAREN KELLOCK 102

KAREN KELLOCK PH.D.

Manual for Superior Men

A complete theory based on Einstein physics, Political Psychology, Systems Theory and Archetypal Psychiatry.

FORMULA
**All success attraction
All disease obstruction
All recovery elimination**

**You must fast on all three
OBSTRUCTIONS:
People
Habit
Food**

KAREN KELLOCK 102

People: they'll advise you wrong and say it's ok to sin. They want you down so they can take over friend. You're a person of substance and they have nothing inside to assist--only to resist. Depending on life-level they have demons see so stop taking advice and do your own thing. For we're fighting principalities and powers not people but eliminate em anyway, they're evil. We must resume our Puritan roots of not trusting so easily. Tried, tested, proven--see?   Once free we're happily in synchronicity and flow with the SPACE for sudden growth.

KAREN KELLOCK 102
Author's Notes '23

DESIRE FOR PRIVACY THWARTED
DANGEROUS ORATION
THANK HIM FOR PAINFUL LESSONS
BEEN THRU IT: EMPATHY DEVELOPED
INCITING RIOTS AND DIVISIONS
THE NOTION OF TOTAL LOAD

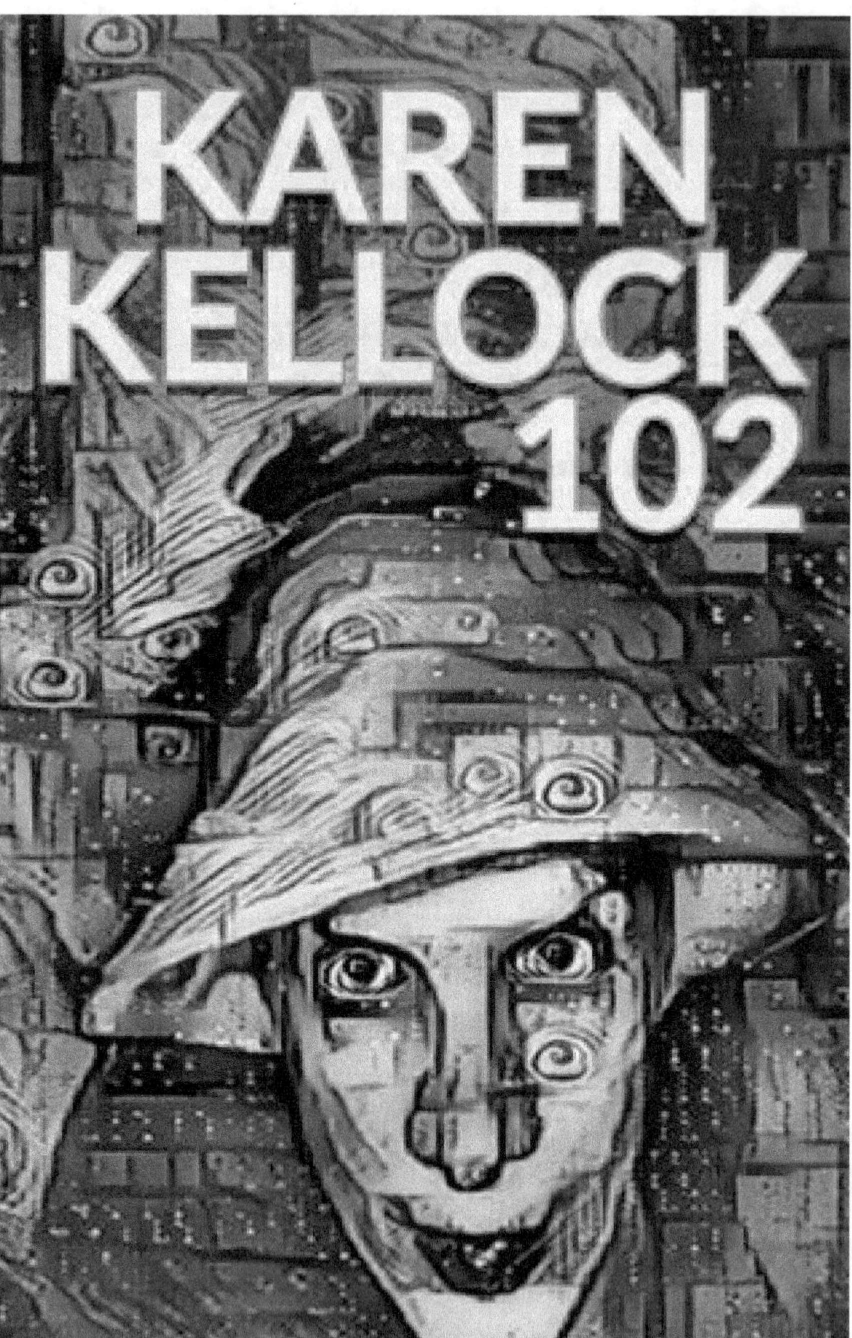
KAREN
KELLOCK
102

KAREN KELLOCK 102
Author's Notes '23

We may see the bible as a war manual. That's how Constantine saw it after many wins in battles.

Unforgiveness locks us into time and place. Bad memories become anchors to disgrace.

Let your PTSD memories give you strength in your armor and no more--let it make you a warrior.

You're STILL terrified at the sudden changes in their reactions to you, you're a fallen hero too.

Because he told them they were superior they woulda done anything for him, their Fuhrer.

Being suddenly trapped with the bully in the family was the experience scarring them for life see.

I love The Rifleman when Lucas can mow em down from the hip cuz he practiced with 1000 hits.

DESIRE FOR PRIVACY THWARTED

They act like there's something wrong with wanting privacy like as if you hate people see.

Impulse control/emotional regulation doesn't happen 'til age 25 so choose one after that, aye.

The same things that made him peculiar to people made him charismatic to millions: good vs evil.

Tho' he seems lost and directionless, inside he's doing something important for mankind, honest.

Inside him is a fertile anarchy of ideas which eventually mold together in new and bold matrices.

She was like a tired stray dog who'd throw in her lot with anyone showing kindness: danger or not?

Latent ideas begin to crystalize: that's the sequence building a new personality which is real, aye.

Becoming sure of latent beliefs is a milestone in the personality: BOLDNESS gets results see.

DANGEROUS ORATION

Some aren't happy unless inciting riots and divisions. When things are tranquil she has tantrums.

Hitler was so powerful he could orchestrate millions. There's power in good and bad positions.

The kings collude together against GOD'S MAN. The first page in Psalms says it man--hold on.

The Creative Act: just START and you're carried along in a stream until you're done and it's over.

We must free you of HER BAD influence--tho' he never had any problem: think Hitler's voices.

A speaker like Hitler is like a magnet being passed over people's heads: a calling, a pulling ahead.

Hitler: the more adulation he got the more hate-filled he was. Interesting how that works today alot.

I was invaded to learn boundaries. Only invasion built the social muscle I needed for a lifetime see.

How to deal with PTSD: Thank God for the vital but painful lessons building your boundaries.

Don't worry, if you use your new assertion this will never happen again, the disaster way back when.

Turn that deep pain of PTSD memory around to build boundaries so it never happens again see.

THANK HIM FOR PAINFUL LESSONS

Thanking God for painful lessons turns everything around to seeing silver linings/acceptance.

You were a sitting duck before as sharks smelled blood in the water with no protection whatsoever.

You were unprotected, a naive little girl. You're hep now so just relax--life is a ladder so it's over.

The biggest lesson I got after the invasion was I wanted them. Take responsibility: you were lonely.

Having been sheltered I never learned boundaries and no one ever told me "don't let em in" see.

His creeping invasiveness matched your weaselly weakness and that's the system so forget it.

You're still terrified cuz a bigger/dominant force took you over. A group of kids, the girls, whatever.

A group of kids whose brains haven't developed without impulse control: that's BIGGER than y'all.

BEEN THRU IT: EMPATHY DEVELOPED

I understand it cuz I've been through it: treachery, betrayal, leaks, calumny, collusion, twits

They saw you as disgusting when you wouldn't go along with them see. You took it as truth/disease.

Cuza all I went thru being cast aside by you I turned it around to TOTAL success in all I pursue.

I can write about the game cuz I'm no longer in the running. I can see it but God's protecting.

There are those who can't create the future cuz they can't get over the past: grudges no less.

Paul saw the hardest thing as his greatest achievement: to forget the past so the future proceedeth.

INCITING RIOTS AND DIVISIONS

Hitler: "We must free the German people of their enemies" tho' they didn't know they had any.

Oration: Hitler could speak/express the anger everyone felt as well as blaming someone else.

It is a small, rootless international clique that is turning people against each other. Adolph Hitler

Hitler's intolerance was taken as strength of character. The more riots he incited the stronger.

Predictably, it was BEER halls in which Hitler gained most prominence for hating various foes.

Hitler's masterfulness in inciting riots in people reflect the serial bully's in a family spreading evil.

In hix politix it started: Give em beer, make em mad and incite hatred against a foe calling em bad.

He spoke from the heart to all of us. He made things conscious that we all felt. Hitler youth

Charisma does not exist on its own in anyone. It's an interaction between the audience and one.

Hitler told the audience what they wanted to hear, that they were WAY superior/hurt by inferior.

When in misery people long for a charismatic leader see. Lead us out, give us relief from treachery!

German history was rich in stories of such heroes. That's often all it takes with the resentful.

THE NOTION OF TOTAL LOAD

Cure for dander allergy: control diet to lower total load and get air purifiers for all rooms—it's easy.

Millions die of choking yearly cuz they ate dinner see. Best not to bring that up at a dinner party.

Hitler had digestion issues and was flatulent. This made his dinner parties intolerable I'll bet.

Shortbread: Flour from wheat, sugar from cane, butter from cow and that's all: no soy/adulterants.

I'm done with my work and retirement comes first. Now I'm looking at snow falling to the earth.

Just when it becomes effortless you become famous for it. It's as easy as pie now, they'll love it.

The rocketlauncher and production manager is coming, just prepare for the visitation and anointing.

Dog shelters over the country are filled to capacity cuz immigrants get on buses and leave em see.

Please, adopt a dog. He didn't ask to come here to freeze or starve. Don't they care I asked God?

KAREN KELLOCK 102

REFUSE ADVICE YOU NEVER ASKED FOR
HOPE IS POSITIVE EXPECTATION *EVERY* MINUTE
GOD'S CHILDREN ARE NOT A DISEASE
RESISTANCE BUILDS MUSCLE
FALLEN CHURCHES ARE WORLDLY/BORING
JEZEBEL HELL
HIX HATE GENIUS
LEVELING INSTINCT OF QUEEN'S MAIDS
THE COMMUNIST SPIRIT LEVELS YOU
KIDS ARE WASHED OUT, SILENT AND INDECENT
SELF-RIGHTEOUS RAGE ACTIVISM
THINKERS AND INTROVERTS
HYPERSENTIVE BRAINS ARE WIRED DIFFERENT
WE. CAN'T OPERATE ON THEIR LEVEL!
NO SMALL TALK OR UNNECESSARY DISCUSSIONS
EMOTIONS AND SENSITIVITY ARE GENETIC
INSULATION FROM PEOPLE BRINGS WORLD SUCCESS
"FRIENDS": GENERATION OF CHAOTIC NOISE
ARCHETYPAL REACTIONS AND REJECTIONS
GOD'S SUPPORTERS ARE READY
ONCE THE CLUTTER'S GONE
THE PAST IS DEAD WEIGHT/LAW OF AFFINITY
RESISTANCE BUILDS MUSCLE
DAM DEMS AGAINST AMERICANS
TREACHEROUS MS. SPEAKER
DAM DEMS WILL BOOMERANG
DAM DEMS AND HIX POLITIX
IN BRITAIN NO JUSTICE/IT'S SERIOUS

KAREN KELLOCK 102

KIDS: DON'T TAKE EM IN
CHILDREN OF ANGRY MOTHERS
SCAPEGOAT SYSTEMS AND IDENTITY
SERONTONIN IS DOMINANCE, SRI's MOUSINESS
MILLENNIAL SCUM LOVES HOLLYWOOD SCUM
SHUT UP AND GET OUT
DECEITFUL PEOPLE LOVE SCAMS OF MANIPULATION
WHITE NATIONALISTS THEY CALL US
MADNESS OF CROWDS—WHERE'S IT COMING FROM?
THE MADNESS OF SOCIAL JUSTICE AND ONENESS
FINDING THE INCORRECT AND TELLING IT
SICK SYSTEMS SIDE AGAINST ONE
LET TOTAL SOLITUDE EDUCATE EM
DARE TO DISCIPLINE NOT LISTEN TO EM
MY GOD WAKE UP MAN
LEFTIST RADICALS HATE AMERICA
BIDEN CORRUPTION
NATIONALISM IS MORAL
TRUMPISM ALL OVER THE WORLD
ANOMIE--NORMLESSNESS
DIVERSITY IS GOD, MAKING GOOD HAPPEN?
PAGAN INTRUSION
SHUP UP DURING THE MOVIE!
THEY MEAN NOTHING
NO, I DON'T WANNA GO ANYWHERE!
PEOPLE AREN'T THAT IMPORTANT
AVOID ALL BAD DRIVERS
ELIMINATION IS RECOVERY/RECOVERY IS ELIMINATION

KAREN KELLOCK 102

UNIVERSAL EXISTENTIAL LONELINESS
OLD FREIGHT'S GOTTA GO
OLD GHOSTS RULING YOUR DAYS
REMOVE ALL INTROJECTS
CONSEQUENCES OF INFERIOR BONDING
BUFFERING AND LOOPING LONELINESS
CHURCH SOCIALS AREN'T GOD
CHURCH OF WOKE WON'T LISTEN TO FACTS
DEMOCRATS WORK FOR ILLEGAL ALIENS NOT CITIZENS
QUICK TRUTHS
MAKING FAMOUS OR PERFECTING SKILLS?
THE GREAT WORK
A PAINTER PAINTS, A SINGER SINGS
PATIENCE IS: HOLDING BACK STRENGTH
ELIMINATION IS KEY TO RECOVERY
STREAMLINE YOUR LIFE
COLLEGE BLOCKAGE AND SRIs
THE BIG UNBRIDGEABLE DIVIDE
GOD DOES THINGS SOONER THAN EXPECTED
STORM SURGE PRECEDED BY SILENCE
DECREASE IS A SIGN OF PROPULSION AHEAD SOON
SUDDENLY...
TERROR OF THE WORLDLY
TROUBLES IN LIBERAL LAND
ESCAPE TO DESERT WILDERNESS
HOPE: SOMETHING GOOD'S ABOUT TO HAPPEN
RESTORATION IS THE WHOLE THING
THE PIT VS. YOUR DREAMS

KAREN KELLOCK 102

DEALING WITH THE COMMUNIST SPIRIT
ELIMINATING PEOPLE OBSTRUCTIONS
OLD FREIGHT/DEAD WEIGHT
POSTMODERN STUNTS
SYSTEM COOLING IS PALPABLE
THE WICKED ARE LIKE CHAFF
PSALMS SAVED ME IN THE WILDERNESS
FAKE CHRISTIAN WOMEN
GOOD, EVIL AND CIVILIZED
FAVOR MAKES YOU LIMITLESS
THE SHALLOW ARE UNFAITHFUL
THE LORD IS MY CHAMPION AND SHIELD
NARROW GATE: FEW FRIENDS
THE TABLES HAVE TURNED, IT'S THE LORD
CULTURAL PSYCHOLOGICAL CRISES
OUR FOES AS CHAMPIONS
SAVING PSALMS IN MEMORY
REVELATIONS ABOUT FOOD
THE AMERICAN BREAKFAST
EARLY NIGHTS AND PERFECTING SKILLS
BOLDLY TELL THE TRUTH NOW
GOD NEEDS NO LITERARY AGENTS
WOLVES IN SHEEP'S CLOTHING
HIGH ORDER/BORDERS EQUALS DISGUST
CREATIVITY NEEDS MATURITY
OVERCOMING LIBERAL INFLUENCES
RETURN TO FIRST NATURE
LAND WITHOUT JUSTICE

KAREN KELLOCK 102

REFUSE ADVICE YOU NEVER ASKED FOR

They'll advise you wrong and say it's ok to sin. They want you down so they can take over friend.

You're superior but can't feel it since they've taken you over sucking you dry and I want this over.

You're a lady/man of substance and she has nothing inside to assist only to tear down: RESIST.

I'm so relieved I never have to see em again. Pained memories, I can't believe I didn't see it then.

Depending on life-level people have demons in em. Stop taking their advice and do your own thing.

It wasn't you it was the demons in you so stop this remorse and thank God they are now gone.

For we're fighting principalities and powers not people but get rid of em anyway, they're evil.

We must return to the Puritan way of not trusting people so easily. Tried, tested, proven—see?

Once free of people problems we can have a happy life in synchronicity and flow in just us ya' know.

People-elimination will create a SPACE for sudden explosive growth, so now finally here we go!

HOPE IS POSITIVE EXPECTATION *EVERY* MINUTE

Hope is the positive expectation that something good can happen at any moment.

For victory we must know God **WANTS** our healing--make that switch, not always wondering.

Don't pray "if it be Your will" cuz you already know it is. Take **HIS** will to the throne with boldness.

The closer we get the more silent He is. Is this a test? Perhaps--of faith and fidelity I guess.

He must test our faith and these are the dry silent years of nothing happening, a fearful space.

We must make the switch from wondering to knowing His will: of victory and total healing.

It's not gonna happen right away--the **WAITING** period is a necessary test of faith, ok?

He **WILL** do it, He **WILL** do it...cuz His word says He will and that's all I need to know to be sure of it.

GOD put all that in me, all those words flowing out effortlessly, so I know He'll bring the victory.

Confirm your identity to yourself and others: You are perfect but fighting a temporary disease/addiction.

You were crazy at times, who wasn't? It's just that you stuck out like a sore thumb/unpleasant.

GOD'S CHILDREN ARE NOT A DISEASE

You are **NOT** that disease or state of being. It's subject to change cuz your God is moving.

Temporary: I learned what I needed in a desert shack then God moved me to a house so slick.

God **WANTS** my victory, He said I'd prosper in whatever I do and He'd make sure of it too.

It's a scary thing when religion becomes a business and churches become worldly and diminish.

When a church gives donkey rides or other amusements you know they're lost too.

The fallen church does cute skits and worldly amusements clearly showing they've lost it.

Confirm your identity to yourself and others: You are perfect but fighting a temporary thing--cancer.

All have struggles in fact it seems they are constant but that's life as we overcome obstacles.

RESISTANCE BUILDS MUSCLE

I'm always stronger for it, I always end up saying I'm much better because I went thru it, so thanks.

My biggest lesson: don't go off with people. Losing independence till I'm back home is not regal!

Mean men will leave you off somewhere, mean women will detain you with social affairs.

When you're in someone's car you're a captive to all their stuff, their ideas and THEIR decisions.

And besides, do you know how they drive? Be sure you vet that before EVER getting in, no jive.

He said I was rude not letting him in without calling first but he was rude to invade privacy--cursed!

The devil is real dear--I know cuz I kept company for so many years--so you must avoid nonbelievers.

The more debauched Trailer Trash Tammy becomes the more they love her then she gets worse again.

You couldn't be so far up now had you not been so far down then, so stop remembering/remorsin'

FALLEN CHURCHES ARE WORLDLY/BORING

The minute I walked into the "Christian" church it was more like a loud social affair, a curse.

Unruly kids running around yelling, parents trying to get the best social seating, it was total bedlam.

The years of fighting the devil and still being in denial are coming back to me and it's phenomenal.

These say it's not "nice" to say "slut"—but it's ok to be one, *what*?

Why would it take 40 years for denial to lift? That's how possession works-- reprobate mind adrift.

Sin is true possession, I can attest to it. Lost years I'll never get back but I'll make the best of it.

HIX HATE GENIUS

We're all sinners and ALL have sinned. For an artist only repentance releases success and wins.

Beethoven had to put up with persecution in small towns especially from children who hated him.

Worst abuse is being demeaned and misjudged because you're a genius/I can attest to this.

God's wrath is dystopia: terrible life condition coming from deprivation, oppression or terror.

They use it as a means of birth control and these women have become so callous, dear Lord!

God disciplines like an angry Father at times, that's what it takes with obdurate appetites/crimes.

To learn about the world and boundaries, I had to deal with a gang of J.D.'s and it was scary.

I learned about boundaries and borders real fast, invaded by losers while being a good hostess.

I went to the store and when coming back, a buncha people lying on the floor! Disorder, bedlam, bores.

JEZEBEL HELL

Jezebel wants a man who will "fight" for her [not just protect her] to perform vengeance on her foes.

Don't get close to a Jezebel with her strong man cuz he'll come against you on her command.

His nasty vengeance on you the innocent is him "fighting for her"--hear that and reject her.

Haven't you noticed all her men rose up against you unexpectedly? She was the author probably.

She's a nasty evil woman who will stop at nothing to get vengeance and she uses her men to do it.

You'll find your pet missing or dead cuz Jezebel sent her man on a mission for rejecting the she demon.

By her doing that--robbing you blind--it means she won't come back so thank our God for it.

She's a "loving" phony with her little memes but there's nothing behind it, she's dumb as beans.

Just stay away from me, I've graduated--I don't need a Jezebel in my life I'm sick with hatred.

All you have in you baby is thousands of souls being a slut and that makes you a haunted house.

Your friendship meant all your buds advising me as if I asked em for it, it was degrading you nut.

All your friends knew he/she was a creepy interloper but not you--why was this, question it too.

Well don't get sucked in again. There are losers and Jezebels all over and you gotta be ready friend.

She gets vindictive when she's low or a little restless, that's when she comes over and makes a mess.

If you don't have firm boundaries the world will crowd in and life will never be the same, amen.

Don't let her in or it's all about HER choices cuz that's the Jezebel, taking over with lowness.

Jezebel would sic her sex enslaved men on me--she used em like a sheriff, enforcer or gun see?

The slut is a haunted house of all the men and all their mates/spouses so they're losers/louses.

Feminists confuse men's desire for achievement/competence with patriarchal desire for tyrannical power.

MEN are the most seriously hurt: in prison, on the streets or victims of violence/suicide/wars.

Men are most seriously hurt so where is the male dominance? Things are getting worse cuza this.

LEVELING INSTINCT OF QUEEN'S MAIDS

It was the Queen's maids putting her down about her age through their unkind lyrics as they played.

My house is small enough that I can do everything my self cuz I don't want em here, the "help"!

The housekeeper resented me cuz I was the owner and caused me much disorder so we fired her.

It's the communist spirit, the leveling instinct--the maid degrades great genius with her rinky dink.

Maid announced she broke my mirror--how symbolic about Queens brought down by jealous hers.

I don't want them back in my house EVER. Guard the hearth with your life, these are SPIRITS that enter.

She brought all her little kids running around opening closets and drawers, laughing at us owners.

THE COMMUNIST SPIRIT LEVELS YOU

Never ask em to order your basement cuz half will be gone--they just take it cuz they want it, oh God!

No character has been taught to children. They just take it cuz they want it and to hell with you friend.

Dunning-Kruger: Losers thinking they're superior and it's all about robbing/degrading the owners.

In the 3rd Reich professors were chosen as best in their field but most importantly: totally RELIABLE politically.

All explanations of California Fires are climate change, not liberal refusal to invest in infrastructure--strange.

California and all liberal states are not about infrastructure etc. but about social justice programs: get this.

Burning down California to prove climate change? Cuz that's the only explanation given--it's green communism.

KIDS ARE WASHED OUT, SILENT AND INDECENT

Just cuz the kids are washed out and silent doesn't mean they're decent, get a grip about this.

FOX IS GONE. Only Tucker, Hannity and Laura remain as sane and 100% on Trump Train.

GLOBAL standards for the treatment of dogs means NO standards for the treatment of dogs.

A kid can be washed out and silent but still house demons cuz entry points are omnipresent.

The washed out and silent girls indecently put fecal on the walls in covert rebellion, get rid of em.

Other than "help us manage" pray "Lord I know you WANT to heal us, Your plan is bigger than this".

Lost years cycling thru my memory bank, one layer at a time as I face my crimes that went blank.

SELF-RIGHTEOUS RAGE ACTIVISM

Self-righteous rage activism is already backfiring on environmentalists cuz we've had it with this.

They think unhinged hysterical environmentalism will work, stirring up the masses I guess.

Liberals lay blame for climate change at our feet while saying we can be saved by globalist cheats.

To insulate from people was like getting out of jail, the constant mental impositions equaled fail.

The officious and invasive questions, contradictions and the great/thankless effort it takes to bond.

THINKERS AND INTROVERTS

Why does cerebral mean absentminded? Because life is a PIE--you're either here or there, absorbed in it.

I just wanna be alone to think--and everything else comes around that.

It's not that I can't do anything about it, but that I won't make a move without God's permission.

Spending time with God is the only way bondages can be broken, it sets us free, it's fun. Joyce Meyer

Hypersensitive: a very deep processor, acute emotions and avid appreciator of little things usually unnoticed.

As a hypersensitive I couldn't enjoy or tolerate the same activities as my peers, they bored me to tears.

As a sensitive introvert I stopped dating cuza the sex that was expected of me, like refusing marked me crazy.

The casual sex expected in hookup culture is an invasion of privacy, sickening, hauntingly meaningless, a hex.

If you wanna read a person listen to their words. Porn culture spreads like wildfire, divide from the tares.

HYPERSENTIVE BRAINS ARE WIRED DIFFERENT

The brains of sensitive people show increased blood flow to areas processing emotions, awareness, empathy.

Being offended by a seemingly harmless, offhand remark from a friend or colleague--yah, that's all part of it.

HIGH sensory sensitivity to external stimuli, emotional reactivity and cognitive processing = always thinking!

The fact that I was always thinking made em mad. They wanted me doing their thing like peas in a pod.

A careless heckle from a stranger can leave us emotionally shaken for days or we feel a sting of conscience, ok?

When seeing beautiful things or kids running to their parents I tear up with little control over it.

William James calls it the "gift of tears" of the saints. I can relate to that, I've cried for days.

We are very creative, attuned to little subtleties and a richness in things that others may overlook.

WE. CAN'T OPERATE ON THEIR LEVEL!

Hypersensitives draw inspiration from our complex inner lives to create beauty, joy, and inspiration for others.

Hypersensitives are incredibly conscientious and take great pride in their tasks--only once you have to ask.

They work hard so it's done right are great employees if they have autonomy, space, and time to ponder.

Hypersensitives feel more deeply. While this can be wild if they're maudlin they also feel the heights of ELATION.

Because they're in tune with the lesser-noticed things in life they worry about animals/how they are handled.

As hypersensitives we feel far more passion for a topic and can actually burst with enthusiasm, explosive.

I'm sorry I just can't fake an interest in topics, people, tasks, and activities that don't suit me cuz life is a PIE, see?

Life is a pie man--I wanna leave time for things I find fulfilling: people and tasks of my OWN choosing.

Superior man knows he rises high above the masses so he waits, works on himself and anticipates miracles.

Driven by an inner search for meaning, they can't do the meaningless anyway--they must silence or filter it out.

NO SMALL TALK OR UNNECESSARY DISCUSSIONS

They loathe small talk and unnecessary discussions because really, who has time for that? Minions.

Sensitives will continue working on a mental problem until solved, not "out of sight out of mind" like with most.

The hypersensitive hates open office plans and desires to work in a closed, private, calm environment.

The hypersensitive hates chaos foremost and in loud environments will run and hide, often terrified.

As sensitive empaths we despise violent movies and are bored with extreme use of effects or too much sex.

I don't like presenting to an audience cuz I can feel and hate their watchful eyes--it's these things I despise.

After a long day I need solo, quiet time to recharge and that means NO ONE: even my beloved husband, depart!

Congratulations! We're a club of deep-thinking, creative doers who need a LOT more quiet time than most.

A highly sensitive person means you process sensory data more deeply than most so to them good riddance.

How does a sensitive empath handle a blockhead family who mocks and misjudges his fine traits?

His parents say he's "over-reacting" by having feelings-- dreamer, a spoiled brat with delusions of grandeur.

The children are raised with emotional neglect--non-response to their emotions--creating emotional illness.

Refusing to value their emotions especially for young hypersensitives creates unhealthy outcomes.

Emotional neglect has higher impact than abuse but is not as memorable or noticeable as physical abuse is.

Kids feel like their needs aren't important, their feelings don't matter and asking for help is a weakness.

Emotional neglect becomes unnecessary guilt, anger, low self-confidence and a sense of being deeply flawed.

EMOTIONS AND SENSITIVITY ARE GENETIC

Emotions are a hypersensitive person's first language--but his family may not speak that language or bash it.

High sensitivity is a genetic trait: You're either born with it or you are not--with emotional neglect he's still got it.

They divorce themselves from the most important part of their sensitive child's inner life: emotions.

It's like being a musician in a world with no music or having parents who actively tell you your music is bad.

The feelings of a deeply thoughtful, intense child are ignored or discouraged--viewed as a weakness.

That kind of emotional neglect sends sensitive children a message: Your greatest strength is not valued here.

INSULATION FROM PEOPLE BRINGS WORLD SUCCESS

It would have to be so good, so magnetic, so otherworldly and godly I couldn't resist it.

You can't get to this level, top of your game and life's culmination and not need solitude to pursue it.

The more energy you have the more parasites come in to thieve it and that's lesson #1: believe it.

As a single woman I felt I didn't have the right to do this cuz thieves came in to capture me quick.

They wouldn't leave me alone! It was as if I didn't have a right to solitude by anyone I knew.

But that was the first half of life, my boot camp about people and the True Psychology of Man.

Now I'm in my REWARD life after learning these lessons and now I have NO interruptions.

I work all day and night cuz my husband protects my solitude and privacy and no one gets in even him.

People don't realize their wasted lives in these social things without which life is SO rich and inspiring.

My inner life is infinite castles to explore. My outer life is the beautiful red mountains I adore.

"FRIENDS": GENERATION OF CHAOTIC NOISE

Outer dramas were SO hectic, hurtful, treacherous and miserable I escaped inside to the ineffable.

When I die I can't take a million friends with me. This friend fetish of liberals is a wasted destiny.

TV "Friends" shows this: a crowded apartment and constant talking while destiny is missed. BORING

Chaos is the operating system for Millennials cuz it's seen as freedom and order is too old fashioned.

Chaos is freedom: that's "self-expression" without rules or even ethics cuz boundaries they reject.

First you get the women, then the children, then follow the men. Adolf Hitler

It's a budget or a pie: You cannot have your destiny if crowded out by thoughts of years gone by.

ARCHETYPAL REACTIONS AND REJECTIONS

They treated you badly due to sins, a natural reaction. It's not humanity but sin's dark passions.

After what you went thru you hate sin too so don't hate those who hated your sins tho' few.

Revulsion against sin is an archetypal reaction to a lowminded caricature: with sin there's no allure.

They're reacting to a dark archetype recognized on a primal level: these are brain stratas, literal.

You throw out a dark archetype like that, all hell breaks loose and in like kind you get it back.

We perceive thru the archetypes. All behavior becomes caricatured into love or fights.

Telling the truth can bring these archetypal reactions because it's seen as evil in dense generations.

GOD'S SUPPORTERS ARE READY

God has supporters ready but if they sense you have baggage, are messed up or a burden they'll run.

If you have crap weighing you down it's negativity--positive people wanna move not be with kiddies.

Great stuff starts happening easily if you are LIGHT WEIGHT with nothing burdening or irritating.

You gotta be ready to go at a moment's notice, flexible, pliable and bold when God says "Yes".

Are you ready with your original stuff or still copying others? Cuz that'll always be third rate/obvious.

Pastors design sermons from my stuff but that's ok because I'm a theoretician and it's not a bluff.

It wasn't so much that he was multi-talented but that the Renaissance spirit had taken over him.

The Renaissance Man is busy every moment putting things where they belong and eliminating wrong.

When the clutter's gone you can start to see the road, your path in life. Only then, or you die.

Once you eliminate the stuff/past holding you down the rest comes easily until you're full blown.

ONCE THE CLUTTER'S GONE

Once you're successful with power to do anything you want, THEN you can help the world out.

If you're good they'll want to support you but if messed up they'll quickly/definitively drop you.

People treated you badly but back then you deserved it--that's facing your sins with humility.

You sin, God's wrath is poured out thru people. You repent, now God turns his wrath on their evils.
Looking back it's simply unbelievable all you did cuz that's the demons: unpredictable and ridiculous.

There's no explaining demon's actions so the past is a mystery no matter how much you return to em.

The past was just the meeting of the archetypes--your lowness loved his lowness and the like.

The mere fact you were doing that means you had to face a big fat angry mean harridan in your face.

You gave a lower archetype and that triggered the punishment and our God users actors for that.

Once trying to escape Satan ropes you back in with **THOUGHTS** that stream by--refuse em/bye.

Victimized twice: the incident [robbed, raped, mugged], then thoughts about it [mind-fogged].

THE PAST IS DEAD WEIGHT/LAW OF AFFINITY

My low life level as an addict attracted his low life level as a user of women, invader and sadist.

Mate-selection is not random but exact. Despite my titles, if dense I attract creeps and sad sacks.

If happens subconsciously: the law of affinity. Like tones vibrate together, we understand each other.

To attract the link for success out the gate you gotta go **LIGHT WEIGHT**/get it all in a bag ready mate.

I've done this great and marvelous work and wonder yet I go back to the past which steals my thunder.

RESISTANCE BUILDS MUSCLE

No matter how bad the past it helps to see how your biggest foe gave the resistance to build muscle.

She made me so crazy always blocking me, I got better and better until I was strong/amazing.

Always putting me down like I was no good fired me with ambition to disprove her and be understood.

Seeing it all as a necessary bootcamp dissolves the resentment that could potentially hold you back.

Because I had weak boundaries I had to be imposed on for years to de-enmesh myself from peers.

There is a devil and people do monstrous things under his influence until it's gone/exorcized.

DAM DEMS AGAINST AMERICANS

Everything is projection with them. When Trump attacks back they always call it "intimidation".

The left are afraid because their power is lessening with every deal by Donald Trump. Jon Voight

When Trump said "You've a lovely country--shame if anything happened to it" they called him Mafia.

Democrats are so possessed with anti-Trump rage they're incapable of doing anything but hate.

The election will be between the dem's revenge and resistance politics or President Trump's RESULTS.

If something is "human-centered" it's not God-centered but globalist, progressive and weird.

It's unprecedented in American history for a speaker to initiate impeachment with no evidence at all.

Speaker starts impeachment without saying what the crime is or even reading the report it's based on.

Satan, the author of the bad wretched past, knows exactly what to bring to your mind for stress.

That's why you must control your mind now for it's true that if empty it's the devil's playground.

They can't name a high crime or misdemeanor--it's all based on here-say, the usual liberal behavior.

TREACHEROUS MS. SPEAKER

Pelosi is going against the American people who elected and WANT Donald J. Trump--so evil!

Pelosi isn't a leader she's a follower--of AOC, a buncha kids' fanbase, liberal feminist idiots.

All we've seen here from Ms. Speaker is a perpetration of a fiction and they oughta fire her.

Dam dems and Pelosi can't stand the fact Trump's leading and that he's doing great things.

No evidence just hear-say, rumor and innuendo--that's how she wants to run government? No.

Corporate global social score/corporate banking--so dangerous and it's over everything.

Indictments are there, it's coming and all hell's about to break loose cuz they cooked their goose.

Antifa to shoot up theatres: Chicom revolution-starting crap. The pentagon knows about it.

Why would we forfeit the power we've got and our history just so globalists can piss all over us?

The now-woke pentagon's decided it's not gonna just sign over to the Chicoms for no reason.

The pentagon's decided it's not gonna sell out America and piss all over our forbearers.

It's a chicken crap exercise of chicken-necked nobodies selling America so they can be somebody.

DAM DEMS WILL BOOMERANG

The dems ONLY have a vision of how to ruin this president and overturn the will of the people.

Think I'm kiddin'? It's the women in congress askin' insulting, meaningless questions about nothin'.

Pelosi was clear impeachment was wrong but has now surrendered to the dem's far-left throng.

Trump wants this impeachment fight so bring it on! They struck first now watch the pres. show off.

Now new trends are creeping in--like there's a moral superiority for being black they're implying.

Now it's reparations for gays: but history was hell for all and we can't work out a balance sheet guys.

Due to professional liberals this has accelerated with the speed of light: WHAT you can say or not.

DAM DEMS AND HIX POLITIX

When the debate is lost, slander becomes the tool of the losers. Socrates

What is the limit tyrants will go? Thomas Jefferson rightly said: to whatever limit you will accept.

To see our president take the chains off America is simply breathtaking, what a quickening.
Stands up to tyrants, defends our sovereignty and gets us out of the deep state and endless wars.

Left miscalculated American peeps thinking for 20 years we were intimidated rather than just asleep.

We just wanna promote Americana: When it's free market, family and self-defense it's cornucopia.

To see Trump so unapologetic and in their faces is so rewarding and enlightening we're just elated.

They are so scared now that their long reign of selling off America is being exposed, hallelujah!

There are two ways to restore the republic: through the courts [he tried it] and thru the military, ok?

IN BRITAIN NO JUSTICE/IT'S SERIOUS

In Britain you'll have police at your door if you say there's a difference between trans and a woman.

We are dragged along with new wave cuz it's exceptionally bullying and we just wanna live.

Few can stand up to the bullying which occurs on campuses/offices if you don't go along with this.

The only people who can maintain the line are writers or philosophers without a hierarchy over them.

They became fabulously rich selling off America & wanna take our guns so we can't rebel, hell ya.

Our surrender is over. The one-sided deals are over. The swamp is panicking and Trump's so clever.

Hollywood is anti-American in cahoots with Chicoms, quarterbacked by inhouse traitors like Clintons.

You can't con an honest man. Trump's a straight-up man knowing that's how you stay outa the can.

Dishonest people fall into scams of manipulation, they love it. Not Trump, he's above it.

Kissing each other's ass while they preside over the gangrape of America and now they want out guns?

Finally people are beginning to see they even NEED to defend themselves. This ain't the fifties.

KIDS: DON'T TAKE EM IN

Involvement with wrong people or a pattern of it from low self-esteem can wipe out decades, see?

I was so lost I thought I wanted their presence, in my distress it was a kind of comfort I guess.

Don't take em in cuz if you enforce discipline [quiet!] they'll take it personally and even get violent.

They've been educated under Newspeak: criticizing their behavior means you're calling em freaks.

They can't stand correction and will rebel and think you don't like them then go to war on you man.

Normally a person is corrected and thanks em for it. Nowadays it's an assault and man, you've had it.

Of course you must correct em unless you want total anarchy, robbery, druggies and even rape, see?

And the minute you do your fate is sealed for you cuz these are little hooligans, even the girls.

CHILDREN OF ANGRY MOTHERS

Mothers angry at absent fathers projected onto the children--who resent her but take on her personality.

Sons of angry mothers are attracted to angry women but will leave them cuz they can't handle them.

This reverberation effect through the generations demonstrate systems theory perfectly.

One characteristic of sick systems is tyranny over thoughts and words bringing violence or a curse.

The accepted members all think alike--like peas in a pod--but will react harshly to the misfit as odd.

Members are system-enmeshed and so weak psychologically with little of their own inner reality.

Their fragile identity is against the ground of each other so any change is a catastrophe of war.

A scapegoat system is where tensions are released by projecting onto one-- the patient or victim.

SCAPEGOAT SYSTEMS AND IDENTITY

He is given a bad identity to maintain the sick system and if he grows up they'll deny it or just reject him.

The bad identity--that slot--maintains the status quo or **HOMEOSTASIS** of the system: they need him.

And so when the victim recovers from his illness the system can't stand it and will fight it {trip him up].

They were good relative to you being bad. If you're not bad then they aren't good--understood?

These systems are **NONSUMMATIVE:** the whole paradigm is bigger than the parts, the members.

You have sick systems with the one who's Christian but the outcast comes back to change the clan.

The scapegoat can either seethe with resentment [degrade] or make gold on the incident/forgive.

SEE THE SYSTEM, that's the therapy. Seeing the **WHOLE** is all you need to know and it's easy.

The scapegoat can either spiral down in the fallen hero syndrome or get up again/heal the clan.

All men are sinners but sins of the scapegoat-misfit stand out while the others are ignored.

SERONTONIN IS DOMINANCE, SRI's MOUSINESS

Serontonin brings dominance--taking your place in the world and winning, overcoming, achieving.

SRI's inhibit serontonin bringing subordinate behaviors--they can tell in a minute you're a worm.

One can be achieving and thriving but take an SRI and suddenly he's a loser conniving, begging.

One can take an anti-depressant in her 20's and feel one-down and needy for a few decades.

Going on SRI's is a decrowning. You lose the top of your head, your goals and ethics--like sinning.

He felt duped cuz she was powerful at first but now she's frowsy, fatty, lazy and complains constantly.

Serontonin is superior dominance of wellness, SRI's bring subordinate behaviors like mousiness.

MILLENNIAL SCUM LOVES HOLLYWOOD SCUM

I didn't know I needed a border wall: where this is you, and this is ME--my oasis, paradise, free.

And I thought I had no choice but to let you in. That's how naive I was, hostess to non-friends.

You messed up my life so much coming over all the time--time lost when I coulda been busy/sublime.

They're the hang-out culture. No accomplishments or achievements just shooting the bull, lechers.

Though it all happened half my life ago it's seared into memory like a war when borders are gone.

It took decades to transcend people-worship where darnit, I couldn't be alone but had to do this.

I NEVER wanted to go out and NEVER wanted to go to your party but actually thought I had to.

The social thing is so drilled into us, we actually feel suspect/freakish for not participating in the fuss.

SHUT UP AND GET OUT

Why the hell would I rather be with you than alone, on my throne, in greatest creativity ever known?

I was shocked to see her let hooligans in but her parents were alcoholics I'm now rememberin'

I hated leaving home where my routines, family, safety and things are--every moment was torture.

How could they surmise it'd be more interesting for me to talk to them than to stay home and think?

The social is a boring waste of time compared to the inner journey to the sublime, a gold-mine.

Dear Lord, the clutter, clamor, chaos of this new world! Please fence me in and wall them out.

DECEITFUL PEOPLE LOVE SCAMS OF MANIPULATION

Give me privacy and I can do anything. Fill me with people and I'm blocked with low self-esteem.

The path from shouting meaningless slogans to the shock of seeing the whole happens suddenly.

But most of these toothless losers are inveterate and obdurate--take em in and you've had it.

A rescued dog is always grateful for life but take one of these in and they will steal you blind.

WHITE NATIONALISTS THEY CALL US

America is **NOT** racist or "white nationalist" because 700,000 white men died to free those slaves.

Increasingly there's a war against white people as racist/white nationalists and it is murderous.

We're not "racist". We had a black president elected twice and we freed the slaves after much death.

America's prosperity was not built upon slavery--90% was of the North and the South was lazy.

When I saw him again he was an old bloated pasty man--for him I had carried a torch, so saddened.

MADNESS OF CROWDS—WHERE'S IT COMING FROM?

The madness of crowds come from the contagion of lunacy, acculturation or **AKA** social hypnotism.

In this era the crowd madness comes from **FEAR** of not-fitting which brings violent punishments.

Recall how your siblings or friends treated you when you transgressed in speech, word or deed.

They made you feel small--well it's much worse now. It's mandatory drugging, institutions or jail.

They actually believe that crap so if you don't they will kill, banish and ostracize--and that's that.

There is no middle ground/grey area--you're either OUT or fully in with these insane Americans.

Just as a rescued cat or dog is revived into a beautiful happy pet, so too you'll be God said.

On the way down the fans spit on you. "Who were you to think you could lead us" they spew.

Once being unfairly or cruelly treated by people we put our trust in God, relieved of human evil.

Cuz much of your hurt came from trusting in man when God said trust NO man/ALL are filthy rags.

When a silly/stupid woman is demanding her rights in a shrieking voice she's a fool of course.

But the pastor can't put down people cuz that's not nice. But that's the main thing--see their vice.

It's not about being nice to each other or not offending--saints are told be bold not friendly.

THE MADNESS OF SOCIAL JUSTICE AND ONENESS

Rational scientific findings are kicked in the dustbin replaced by lofty fantasies now ruling mankind.

The attempt is to impose a new religion on the west based on anti-racism/sexism/homophobia etc.

To demonstrate that you are a good person you must show that you are anti-racist and all the rest.

All the social justice demands run against each other and demand we say and believe contradictorily.

Social justice and climate change is a RELIGION with equal piety and the searching for heretics.

LEFTIST RADICALS HATE AMERICA

If you're mentally unstable you'll be driving in the wrong direction or erratically, off the wall really.

Liberalism is at war with reality and that's why we hate it as we watch it inevitably it do itself in.

Wherever they took the guns the crime rate explodes ten times higher: guns are the crime-preventer.

The left and especially the Squad has grown increasingly radical/do not love America, no.

Left rejects Bill Maher for being a dinosaur cuz it's gone way beyond all logic and has lost power.

The news vacillates: what worries us today we don't remember within days. Retire, be happy/amazed.

When I realized the ephemeral nature of news I decided to start enjoying life, just mind-cruise.

Explore/develop unique talents, cuz as God's child the inner is filled with new creative universes.

To live only on the outer WARPS the inner. The outer is crazy so you're a total lunatic adapting that way.

If they snub us, they're toast. You've been so very gracious to us so we love you the most.

When people die they don't come back here--but theories abound of our relations to late dears.

There was a time I thought the outer was IT [I had no inner] in a bland world of chaos and sinners.

The Squad represents the end of the democrat party--they're the best thing to happen, really.

FINDING THE INCORRECT AND TELLING IT

This religion demands finding those refusing to say the correct things, searching em out and telling.

Finding those people who say the incorrect things or things that until yesterday were seen as truth, see?

Those things you always accepted and learned in school are now seen as false/bigoted you fools.

We tried to adapt to it at first as it started slowly but then it was demand after demand in pure lunacy.

It's recent but explosive, spreading from universities across the country down to us dummies.

Why they're scum: white, elderly, patriarchal male culture is the absolute worst according to them.

There's a war on the problem--which is seen to be white elderly patriarchal male culture scum.

Their perennial reply is "we don't have the map of utopia yet, but we're WORKING on it".

The liberals and feminists are purely vindictive when talking about our western societies.

Hillary Clinton your favorite woman wants mass amnesty, mass immigration, mass lawlessness.

We believe in strong borders/low crime, the dems want open borders meaning plenty of crime.

External threats breed internal solidarity. When the threat is gone so too the peas-in-a-pod family.

Before he knew I had money I was just a "dumb bigot" to him then he switched to enemy-friend.

LEFTIST RADICALS HATE AMERICA

If you're mentally unstable you'll be driving in the wrong direction or erratically, off the wall really.

Liberalism is at war with reality and that's why we hate it as we watch it inevitably it do itself in.

Wherever they took the guns the crime rate explodes ten times higher: guns are the crime-preventer.

The left and especially the Squad has grown increasingly radical/do not love America, no.

Left rejects Bill Maher for being a dinosaur cuz it's gone way beyond all logic and has lost power.

The news vacillates: what worries us today we don't remember within days. Retire, be happy/amazed.

When I realized the ephemeral nature of news I decided to start enjoying life, just mind-cruise.

Explore/develop unique talents, cuz as God's child the inner is filled with new creative universes.

To live only on the outer WARPS the inner. The outer is crazy so you're a total lunatic adapting that way.

If they snub us, they're toast. You've been so very gracious to us so we love you the most.

When people die they don't come back here--but theories abound of our relations to late dears.

There was a time I thought the outer was IT [I had no inner] in a bland world of chaos and sinners.

The Squad represents the end of the democrat party--they're the best thing to happen, really.

BIDEN CORRUPTION

This is a game-changer for the democratic party--they're ALL Ilhan Omar now. Laura Ingraham

Liberals care about harm and fairness but not about authority, in-group or purity. Yah that's about it.

Liberals don't recognize Authority, In-group or Purity as legitimate aspects of morality but they ARE.

Liberals aren't into *in-group*--they hate their own race and prefer foreigners and illegal aliens in our face.

Liberals aren't into *Purity*--it sounds too much like sin and repentance when they wanna be "free".

Liberals won't accept your *Authority* even in your own home--they'll try and talk you out of it.

Conservatives value all five moral values the same: in-group, purity, authority, harm, fairness.

This explains why liberals vs. conservatives have such different views: two vs. 5-point morality.

We're split cuz we have fundamentally different moral psychologies beyond our control.

All five moral points are necessary for our survival as a race so the liberal attitude is a disgrace.

NATIONALISM IS MORAL

Globalism raised income all over the world except the working classes in western societies.

Trump situation: His reward for kicking ass is to have people hate him and want to remove him.

To liberals, attitudes towards diversity or immigration is a litmus test for your morality even.

Nationalists see patriotism as a virtue--their country is unique and worth preserving, that's all.

Patriotism: You love your spouse cuz he's yours not because he's superior to all the others.

TRUMPISM ALL OVER THE WORLD

Nationalists have a bond with their country and believe that implies these moral obligations.

They are duty-bound to protect their own people first--that's what nationalism is, sis.

Governments should place their own citizens first not those from other countries--that's morality, Pelosi.

At this point it's **GENES** plus what I've **LEARNED** thru multi-adaptations combining to a **PHENOM**.

There is nothing racist or base about this social contract, Nancy Pelosi [traitor of the century].

A shared sense of identity, norms and history lowers crime and promotes trust, prosperity, generosity.

"I don't like what he said on twitter but am sure glad he said it"--yah because Trump is speaking for em.

I didn't attack you, you attacked me and I fought back--just like Trump and I'm glad he's like that.

You can't fight the swamp and be elegant. Nice doesn't win in Washington with the violent.

Trump is the right man for the job at the right time and that's always how God fights the slime.

They don't wanna know facts about climate change if it misfits their narrative--it's their religion.

ANOMIE--NORMLESSNESS

ANOMIE--normlessness is not a good thing to social psychologists yet it comes from diversity, yuk.

When immigrants want to assume the language and customs of their new land, it's a complement.

With so many diverse groups coming in you can be certain of an authoritarian counter-reaction.

The truth is plain to see: If you want freedom, take pride in your country. Donald J. Trump

If you want democracy hold on to your sovereignty.

They want to win, we want to tie--because we're nice people, but nice is killing us. Bill Warner

All they've said lately is "kill the president" [mean] so of course he's mobilized Marine teams.

DIVERSITY IS GOD, MAKING GOOD HAPPEN?

If you want democracy hold on to your sovereignty and if you want peace, love your nation. PRES

We're asked to believe things we cannot believe that were invented this morning. Douglas Murray

The crazy justice warrior professor said "I don't care about facts--the idea of truth is a white concept."

All big firms now have implicit association tests, implicit bias training, rewiring people even.

Instead of improved performance the firm asks: Have we got enough trans/gays for this task?

Modern Day Trappings: Diversity is god. If you're diverse enough something good happens.

"If we have enough women, something good will happen." Wow, you'd have to be an idiot man.

Increasing women interviewers doesn't increase female status cuz they're so competitive.

It turns out that women are **NOT** dedicated to furthering the sisterhood--who knew?

The more complicated **DIVERSITY** becomes like a cancer, the less the individual is answered.

In the name of social justice we make our societies more unjust, in the name of racism, more racist.

In the name of anti-homophobe we become more homophobic, in the name of trans we are **MAD**.

Those who the gods wish to destroy they first make mad. That explains everything just like that.

PAGAN INTRUSION

Liberals are steeped in the false dogma of interchangeability--that we are replaced easily.

I came from superior Scottish stock then clan was invaded by a foreign element: I was replaced.

It was another culture and god altogether [many gods] and we were made to accept it all.

He was very nice--oh, I'll grant you that. And made big money so the family forgot their great past.

From acceptance of multiculturalism ["the whole world should get together"] to progressivism.

But nice doesn't cut it--what about how animals were treated in his laboratory? I was horrified darnit.

Along with lost Americana is Christian decency not seen in the third world for pets, women, children.

That is my biggest fear of open borders: coarseness, callousness, cruelty to animals--it's lower than us.

Am I saying we're superior? Yes, in the education of the heart and that's a Renaissance thing for sure.

So my great Christian heritage from Scotch evangelist oration was mocked as old-fashioned.

The fact the foreign interloper made big money sealed the deal--we were conquered by evil.

What does Christian and Hindu have in common? Nothing, really--and to compromise dulls our reality.

SICK SYSTEMS SIDE AGAINST ONE

Liberals love hanging with debauched people cuz it gives them a license to live dirty/act like hell.

Obama attempted to sign us over to the Chicoms, deindustrialize and open the borders to Islam.

A sick system sides against one--that's it's whole game. A gang-rape circle is much the same.

The eccentric loner genius is MUTED in this system and if he can overcome that he's succeeding.

The eccentric loner remains isolated since chumming up to him is prohibited and castigated.

In social societies it's about ISOLATING the one cuz having no ties is a hideous punishment to them.

It's not enough to deny you're a sexist, racist or homophobe you must demonstrate it/it's cold.

You must demonstrate this every day and this is where insanity and public embarrassment starts.

When pinned down they don't know what they're talking about, it's just empty slogans they shout.

The sick system sides against one--the "chosen" patient is the victim of this harrowing game.

The members aren't smart they're dumb which is why they hang together in their hatred, it's fun.

If you refuse to believe in the latest, freshest, newest bullcrap you'll be fired, killed, tricked, zapped.

LET TOTAL SOLITUDE EDUCATE EM

If they're a woman or live in Oregon they're probably liberal--you gotta think of these things now.

Too much hugging/kissing seems like lesbianism or something. Yuk, we live in a carnal generation.

I never have to think about writing or forcing it, I can't NOT do it and the worst thing is to lose it.

Part of the reason they fight and abuse is they can't debate the issues so it's serious: resign, refuse.

You don't see possible victory cuz you're looking too low. Wait for God's link it's HIGH and appropo.

That's how they did it in the old days. Cowboys ate once a day and thus they were really skinny.

Let your total solitude be a lesson to everyone you know cuz they know it anyway in their bones.

I'm busy doing God's work. I don't live in your world it's an inner journey of excitement and adventure.

So leave me alone, I gotta stay home cuz I'm busy and nothing out there even interests me.

DARE TO DISCIPLINE NOT LISTEN TO EM

Your parents didn't discipline so out there in the world when they rebelled you couldn't believe it.

Parents didn't discipline cuz they were afraid of you and also of being ostracized by the schools.

And it was terrible having to adapt to you and all you spewed from the fools in the public schools.

Imagine the stuff you agree to--sick, unhealthy degeneracy--but it's all ok cuz it's herd-approved.

You aren't who I thought you were. I see now that you're a dam liberal and shallow to the core.

It was like a long arduous journey through dangerous jungles and peoples seeing me as prey, ok?

MY GOD WAKE UP MAN

My God, wake up man. See it for what it is and then be catapulted up to a whole new dimension.

Stop smoking, it's choking all your potential and you won't be around to enjoy the fruits of it all.

I don't know about all that wine either. Are you a wino, do you anticipate it like others you know?

Are you making yourself famous or just doing your work? One is divine but the other is cursed.

When a church is more like a fair with entertainment and booths you'll know the end is near too.

When a church does SKITS--coming up with things: rather than the Word it's about entertaining.

Just by mentioning it she minimizes it darnit, see the light about these dumbed debauched witches.

The exalted energy of the person when misplaced onto the sensual drive becomes most magnified.

When successful people fail they see it as a challenge--everything's about "creative potential".

The road to success is seeing everything with new eyes. After they dump dirt on you, you rise.

SHUP UP DURING THE MOVIE!

They talk too much, it's boring. Their loquacious or talk around a subject outa fear of triggering.

It only takes me 30 seconds to express my thought and you interrupt me anyway? Hah

Just because it takes only thirty seconds to say something doesn't mean it's a simple thing.

I'm done with the news, you're not giving me a headache anymore or anxiety to the core.

Watching Betty Broderick my favorite cuz it's in San Diego in the 80's: clean, pristine, decency.

Watching Cast a Dark Shadow my favorite cuz it's England in the fifties with dark wood cabinets.

Everyone is normal in these two movies and it takes me back to saner times so I really enjoy these.

Except Betty Broderick of course since she shot her husband--but there's always sinners in all eras.

Stop talking during the movie. Would you do that in a theatre? It's a whole experience, don't be selfish.

It is so aggravating--just shut your mouth during a movie cuz it's a WHOLE experience buddy.

THEY MEAN NOTHING

Don't be ridiculous, forget about them: they mean nothing/was just a short fling, go on to destiny.

The world is transient, gossip-driven, inferior, boring, ego competitive in status-tension and aggression.

I want no part of it. You can travel around if you like and give your events of lies just give me home life.

Rather than letting early life crap block you, how about seeing it as your databank for breakthru?

Yes I was sick/addicted in that era but what I recall is your ugly cruel treatment tho' I deserved it.

You carry a torch all your life and when you see him again it's an ugly old human from all the strife.

Life is hard on people--they should get better overcoming but instead most die after caving in.

NO, I DON'T WANNA GO ANYWHERE!

No I don't wanna go anywhere. The reason you're always escaping is cuz home isn't your kingdom.

Forget about em, don't give it another thought! It's just a split second in eternity and they're all gone.

People aren't that important--GOD is important but the social addiction is all-consuming, amen?

People aren't that important--they come and go, age and die--but God is so keep your focus on Him.

Since they aren't that important stop fretting over something you said or a past offense to them.

Watch who you are around because that spirit will work on you till you'll degrade to the ground.

They don't exist in that state but we immortalize em in our thoughts, making em superior/first rate.

HIGH boundaries and HIGH order = DISGUST. That's the new Social Psychology in the gist.

PEOPLE AREN'T THAT IMPORTANT

People aren't that important--they come and go, age and die--but God is so focus up in the sky.

The reason I don't let you around me is I can't take the abuse and you're too dumb to realize it too.

I learned reality in a shack in the desert separated from the world of confusers and gainsayers.

I made you the offer but will not wait around to anticipate your reaction, I'm way ahead of it now.

No remorse, I see now I had to go thru it all. It's amazing to me what happens after our fall.

The way people treat you when you're down, how they treated even Beethoven like a clown.

Even tho' I deserved it as i look back I will never forget it cuz I got to see what people were like.

And if you know people you can manage em and learn how to avoid the pitfalls of knowing them.

People will **TURN** on you. Loyalty/fidelity were more important in previous generations but not now.

AVOID ALL BAD DRIVERS

Not saying he's a bad driver but an aggressive driver always passing--so much tension, I'll stay home.

A car is not a toy--always passing in and out. I don't wanna wake up amputated in a hospital!

But he IS a bad driver since the riders are terrified and by the time they get home, exhausted.

Definition of a good driver: when the riders can relax and enjoy the ride!

If the devil's in it I'm gonna yell at it cuz I'm the keeper of the hearth in my holy house.

That's the mystical Diana--keeper of the hearth, making sure all is well/moral with her charges.

I have renounced the mediocre world and live in the Great Mind of all geniuses who ever lived.

Women who've had abortions suffer rages later. Divorces, breakups and God's wrath for murder.

Women are filled with arrogant confidence now but study them later: their lives are ruined/silenced.

She was so happily married and lived in cornucopia but after aborting it all turned to dystopia.

Female preachers pacing back and forth over the stage, YELLING like a fish wife in a rage.

ELIMINATION IS RECOVERY/RECOVERY IS ELIMINATION

The more I get rid of the happier I am. More quintessential, more quintessential=freedom!

Being in the presence of God is so humbling: it's love, it's strength, it's all the answers.

Ice cream created rolls within three days--it's either from the sugar or the chemical sequestering.

Watch out for lust because lust brings emotion which cannot be trusted--you don't love that big lug.

Sex blinds the eyes, lust ends in cries, emotion makes you love those you should despise.

Saying "I'm a good person" is the road to hell. You gotta say JESUS CHRIST tho' the world rebels.

Say: "God, make me famous in my field so that I may help people and spread these truths that I know"

Not fame for ego's sake or compensation for family fakes but the amazing new dent you'll make.

Watch who you let in your life because the fakes will be on the take or let your dog out the gate.

My discernment and ability to understand the enemy comes from my relationship with God, not little me.

You must be magnanimous: quick and willing to forgive. Noble and fair, as in a ruler or leader.

There is an existential loneliness we're distracting from which loops into an irresoluble kingdom.

There's an existential loneliness that makes us hang onto others, terrified of a loss or whatever.

To return to that place of emptiness--that haunting place--is tantamount to horror and death.

This profound emptiness experienced as haunting loneliness brought a shut down in early eras.

UNIVERSAL EXISTENTIAL LONELINESS

We should age WITH our loneliness, get into it, learn to appreciate it thru our God-connectedness.

Their course is no solution for not having to feel the groundless, empty universal/normal loneliness.

When there is no heavenly vision of God this loneliness is devastating but if so, it's elevating.

Without people my vision snapped to almighty God and it was a most wonderful release, I'm awed.

God is endlessness and shrewd clever answers we never woulda thought of, the ineffable rod.

This loneliness is not personal but universal--it's not about your flawed mind, falling short or a fool.

This loneliness tho' universal can become clinical depression if there is no God as The Solution.

The clerk smirked and it triggered devastating loneliness--it's that kind of thing, ridiculous.

We are born fundamentally with this gnawing sense of emptiness and being alone, more or less.

We are designed to connect to others: our attachment/nervous system, our brain discovers.

OLD FREIGHT'S GOTTA GO

You can be "in relationship" with a person who's not there. This is not good, it's an introject--beware.

The human ability to maintain relationship with absence provides continuity or can be lunacy.

Don't let an introject--from incomplete mourning or a reject--act as a template or your days are wrecked.

I don't want this holographic hangover from broken relationships blocking my destiny, what a tragedy.

You talk about control, that's it: hangovers of failed relationships determining my day? Forget it.

Don't be controlled by people nor memories cuz that's how they hang around like little demons.

INTROJECTS: People swallowed whole, guiding behavior like ghosts--we must get these out.

OLD GHOSTS RULING YOUR DAYS

A sudden rejection can shock the system to introjection and then a desire for the person.

We don't want these underground games going on. We wanna have total control of ourselves.

Of course there are good introjects but those are integrated as guides not swallowed as aliens.

People are either IN or they're OUT with you man. Learn to discern and stick to that: block, ban.

You've been too hurt, you must rest and relax now--the Art of a Fresh Start is Christian ya know.

What you remember so vividly is just a blurp in eternity or a magnetism of the moment really.

We're not all one we're two but not more than two.

Don't go back, it's too dam dreary. Frightening too cuz you were still in boot camp missy.

Must separate out the power of the introjection paired with rejection—from the real person: scum.

He was scum cuz he made not God central in his life just a buncha "science" concepts, no jive.

Separate out the influence of other people from the power of the True Self they've called dumb/evil.

Dad had to have pig in his gut first thing off cuz eggs, bacon or sausage is American breakfast.

REMOVE ALL INTROJECTS

Demons are real, the devil is real and he will detain you for decades and you won't know it mate.

I'm not gonna let a non-relationship become an introjection guiding my actions, no way man.

That was my last step: remove all introjects so my life could be destiny-directed and perfect.

Despite long periods not seeing you the times I did were horrible and I anticipate life without you.

As long as you've introjected him, you're one-down and on the begging end my friend, it's a hologram.

They did not make God their only source. They made their useless brain the basis of course.

YAH I messed up big time--in that era, that hour, that event, that whatever--but God said "start again".

Our attachment system wants quality bonding and if that's bad the nervous system starts exploding.

CONSEQUENCES OF INFERIOR BONDING

We want to trust our world so we can thrive. When things change like betrayal it caves in from lies.

They see rejections as isolated cases not parts of the whole map cuz their character stinks.

Make me famous in the field/high above the masses cuz I can't stand em rising up against us.

The deep core place longs for connection because we sense this being alone from the beginning.

This lonely groundless homeless feeling is the realm of addiction. You want only to escape it son.

I tried to buffer myself against universal loneliness for years rather than just finally face it in tears.

To avoid loneliness we tether ourselves to identity, groups, events and other ways to connectedness.

With unresolved attachment trauma one is preconditioned to "loop" and latch onto the loss.

We face the illusion of our identity, who we thought doesn't exist, it was all delusion, twisted.

I can identify by what I've achieved, have overcome and by Who's I am/Who I belong to, Jesus.

Who I think I am is made up of memories, stories or habitual thoughts from kids on the block.

If we don't face this universal fear we latch on to "I need a relationship" or that person or whatever.

God will give this world a strong delusion so that they might believe a lie and then be damned.

BUFFERING AND LOOPING LONELINESS

Homesick feeling in gut [of desperate loneliness] was something I'd do anything to cover up.

But the more I evolved the less I could relate at all so the isolation became full, complete, total.

Isolation brought me total joy cuz God's on my side--it's Him I talk to all thru the day and night.

I was desperately lonely in a crowd: phony, chaotic and loud. When alone I was happy with God.

The churches let me down the worst--bricks to carry not lamps to guide--it was boring/I got hurt.

Women run the churches now and you can see the pagan influence, they're falling with style.

Men have learned how to temper power thru the centuries but women may fall into treachery.

Oh sure women work hard and do it all, but the direction is pagan with cute skits for y'all.

Male leaders of old churches held the line, not letting it slip into trendy paganism from the sublime.

Church lady came to my house ragging on me about not going to the socials and I said go home!

CHURCH SOCIALS AREN'T GOD

Your socials aren't God. Your status-climbing in the church is not God. Your chattering is not God.

Christian center deacons and elders were probably picked for social reasons and pure nepotism.

Return to the old paths and you'll be fine--not an entertainment social church which saints flee.

You're a bunch of phonies and I could see it then. Calling yourself loving but a foe not a friend.

You are so empty inside you need constant socials and meetings to make you feel "high" in this life.

The church has booths like a bazaar. Skits and music as man-inspired seems so weird and odd.

I wanted to die to escape outlaw status but then I realized I could start new by shifting my focus.

If a church has become man-inspired it's frightening to the soul--especially when women rule.

Women are always gonna judge emotionally and emotions can't be trusted so it's wrong, see?

CHURCH OF WOKE WON'T LISTEN TO FACTS

If you have ANY views that do not comport with the Church of Woke you're an enemy and evil bloke.

Here's the whole deal: If you don't hold their views you're a heretic and infidel on his way to hell.

There are those who can view reality without an ideological lens vs. those who are totally dense.

Those who are dense will stick to their slogans and NO debate or facts can ever sway them.

That includes most college students--they just won't listen to reason for all the constant brainwashing.

The obdurate sloganizer is the adherent to the Church of Woke and listen they won't.

What we've seen from democrats is a consistent desire/push to impeach regardless of the facts.

DEMOCRATS WORK FOR ILLEGAL ALIENS NOT CITIZENS

Democrats work for illegal aliens, open borders and socialism--we now know these anti-Americans.

Genius is magnification of certain characteristics in problem areas--stretching skills, muscles, materias.

Don't worry about revenge with foes--they're left to their own devices/ will bring themselves down.

Genius is released with EXPANDED SKILLS [MUSCLE] in problem areas [obstacles].

My problem was people always imposing on me so my skills were terse verse to kill the swill quick.

Expecting them to debate is like asking a legless man to run a race. Give up on em in any case.

A 10-day trip took 40 years cuz Israelites couldn't trust God--tried to make it happen themselves.

Whether under Hitler or Mao Tse Tung there's nothing more dangerous than stirred up youth.

That's the way liberals are: they will destroy you if you think differently from them--way below par.

Rise up to focus on God. Transcend people for they're hurtful and saints are seen as odd.

There's not one person on earth who hasn't been hurt by people and life's about overcoming evil.

Since identity is relational their identity depends on you staying down/they'll do anything to forestall.

You've got to agree to all these new orthodoxies or you're cancelled, you're finished, you're toast.

QUICK TRUTHS

I can't create success by chanting, visualizing, voodoo or statements--God decides the minute.

Say it as **CONCISELY**--if it's truth it can be done. But the no-nothing sinner can't be that sure, he flubs.

He talks **AROUND** the subject, he uses his hands. These are tell tale signs of a phony man.

They talk too much, it's boring. They're loquacious or talk around a subject outa fear of triggering.

There is nothing more stultifying than need for herd approval or fear of disapproval: need growing.

The saints are called to be **BOLD** and extraordinary courage in **PUBLIC** marks the saints of old.

I can feel God's hand in everything I write or do. It's simply amazing, like I'm in a wave of bliss too.

These people are creepy and you're a saint. I think it's important that you remember that, aye?

You're now completely harmless and have such tenderness you avoid everything to stabilize.

You've made gold on past envy, you've done your work, you know God'll bring the link, him or her.

MAKING FAMOUS OR PERFECTING SKILLS?

Are you working to make yourself rich/famous or doing work, perfecting skills, purifying soul?

The need for approval/fear of disapproval makes it like you have marbles in your mouth/STOPPED.

It's embarrassing you trying to become famous. It's dense, non-creative, out of grace [disgrace].

You're too attuned to "likes". The herd is crazy yet they're approval of you is all you want--yikes!

It wasn't a huge giveaway gift like they thought, I just got rid of a lot of stuff-- it's their burden now.

After eliminating only the quintessential is left: the most important and appropriate--so you jet up.

A basement full of clothes--are you kidding? They all had spirits in em, I felt "hounded" daily.

They were expensive, perfect, efficient and trendy but I gave em ALL AWAY and feel like a dandy.

What I have left is most efficient/appropriate and nothing else, I am relived of the clothes fetish.

Women think clothes-buying makes them better, prettier, superior or whatever--and it's over.

Because of my compulsive clothes-buying I supplied a whole household of girls who now have style.

THE GREAT WORK

You'll always start where you left off. Just work when you feel like it, like any other art.

To do a huge project, just start with the first one then you're compelled to run through to the end.

Never feel intimidated over the whole, just do the FIRST one then completion to the end is fun.

I'll always catch thoughts on paper and if it becomes a book fine but basically I'm done and retired.

You're finally here, now show them your way is better.

I'm not shootin' for success just to do my best.

I don't go on and on in run-on paragraphs. These are PITHY: succinct, incisive, brilliant, a subtle laugh.

I say it in fifteen seconds and you interrupt me. You take ten boring minutes and no one speaks, see?

The way people never let me get a sentence out was the reason for QUICK TRUTHS to block this.

God put this huge Manual in me of 102 books. I don't know why He did it but all else I have forsook.

A PAINTER PAINTS, A SINGER SINGS

A painter paints, a singer sings, and apparently a writer writes tho' he'd rather do other things.

Five pages daily of quips whether I want to or not. I'm a professional now--I do what I do nonstop.

It'll never work: aspiring to fame and fortune. You must just DO your work and love it to perfection.

Find your true groove and that's all you'll want to do and success will be natural and easy too.

I write because I write. It wasn't always this way I had to overcome, resolve contradictions, fight.

To get em to follow you do your work with **NO** mind to all that stuff and God will provide the rest.

On birthday I realized I was going to die like everyone else--I had a new view after being dense.

It's obvious God comes thru and He supplies the link, for where else could it come from, ya' think?

God'll get em--just like others who tried to hold me back they're gone now, God is my Champion.

PATIENCE IS: HOLDING BACK STRENGTH

The exemplar longs to express himself with the fury and boldness of God and this is his greatest call.

All that held-in fury from oppression without knowin' ya will finally come out hitting its target in America.

Instead of self-pity over bad memories, work em thru then think [ONLY]: I'm done now I can be happy.

You've done your work, wait to be discovered. You're powerful but so subtle only the gem will hear it.

The reward comes when you're reached the point where your work is more important/most fun.

Your work is entirely unique--you've carved a slot for the chic, rewarded when you blocked the freaks.

I decided I'd rather burn with God's enthusiasm for what I'm writing than anger over your treachery.

To calm yourself down, **RETURN** to an earlier time in mind when you were happy, peaceful and calm.

The past crowds in cuz Satan knows how to stop your revolution--in fact you can't even begin.

Your situation was virtuous compared to most yet you're crippled with remorse, that's the saint.

When remorsing over the past you're stepping down and back to lessons unlearned still in fact.

You were different then--you didn't know what you do now so stop going back it's a waste of time.

ELIMINATION IS KEY TO RECOVERY

Seeing your path in life solves depression but how can we see it if cluttered with past aberrations?

We all mess up but Jesus is our safety valve: we can actually start all over again--God of fresh starts!

The past mistakes are erased and a whole new being is replaced and new life begins as God's Ace.

There is no past and anyone who knew it is gone so how does it exist? Those thoughts all my own.

The "Friends" generation of chaotic noise influenced movies with incessant talking and those I avoid.

If socializing is the first priority your utterances are word salad and I want nothing to do with it.

Trying to get approval/avoid disapproval and the biggest fear is out of sync or group's removal.

You were different then--you didn't know what you do now so stop thinking back to the old friends.

Humans screw themselves up with the nonexistent past but animals stay present and have a blast.

Once you've cleaned house, eliminated stuff and banished past you can take that road to success.

STREAMLINE YOUR LIFE

You've got too much--get rid of 2/3 of what you own. Eliminate so you can move forward fast alone.

I gave away 95% of my clothes and kept just the quintessential--feel like a million with so little.

Streamline your life. Make up with your enemies or get rid of them. Start again with **NO** loose ends.

I ordered every drawer and dressed for a visitation from the King at any moment--that's hope amen?

Readiness and absolute preparedness for success to come like a thief in the night as it is promised.

You've completed your work, you gave stuff away, you're stylishly ready now wait for the party.

God blesses the prepared and shiny servants beyond their wildest dreams cuz God is the Extreme!

The whole trick is the **WAIT.** You've planted the huge seed maturing underground until it's great.

The past was just your hard lesson to get to here, a real champion. Why relive it without a reason?

Stop looking for input on the computer--concentrate on your own **OUTPUT** cuz it's the best for sure.   **END**

Tables have turned, that's the point. Don't expect the same bad, it's a new day with God's anoint.

Don't forget while you wait: With your elite art there's only one link for it and the rest may hate it.

COLLEGE BLOCKAGE AND SRIs

Goal of college is not to foster debate but to squelch it: dissidents are crushed, cronies are elevated.

The SRIs they put me on brought regression into decades of immaturity or worse, like a curse.

I was floating thru life, barely surviving and fighting for the right to solitude and finally escaping.

SRIs are two drugs: anti-depressants and anti-psychotics, both will make you sick you nut.

This is how they control the women, most are on anti-depressants and easily brainwashed.

Of course there's a link between Big Pharma and the left which both stand for globalism, to our death.

THE BIG UNBRIDGEABLE DIVIDE

They're no different from their entire generation. When you swim in muddy waters = aberrations.

It was hard to take until I realized why I was ostracized and thru slander cut down to size.

It's happening all over America: family rejection cuza the election and it's a serious civil war beginin'

We're friggin' angry--brother against brother--over this current divide and it's accelerating, so hide.

Worry is like sitting in a rocking chair: We're doing something but it's getting us nowhere. V. Osteen

He called us to be extraordinary--set apart, called by God with unique assignments to do our part.

The problem is our determining God's view towards us by what's going on around us: nothingness!

GOD DOES THINGS SOONER THAN EXPECTED

God is gonna do things sooner than expected--let that take root in your spirit/never feel dejected.

God knows how to accelerate things so you are closer than you think. Not a year but in a blink.

God gives a supernatural surge of favor to lighten the load and take the pressure off--now, not later.

God'll go before you making the crooked places straight--He's gonna smooth everything out, ok?

With God you'll receive breaks you never saw coming and all your problems straightened out suddenly.

Struggling, pressure, weighted down by problems = old life. A new day is coming of ease/NO strife.

Oil makes things unstuck. God will oil our lives so that things are easy, unobstructed, public-loved.

God's gonna make things happen that lighten the load while making you a prince from a toad.

Thank you for anointing of ease, that you're causing me to excel, that you're breathing in my direction.

STORM SURGE PRECEDED BY SILENCE

Storms start by decreasing the tide. Similarly, you may feel WAY decreased before you succeed.

A SURGE of strength, a SURGE of healing--which always happens after a time of decreasing.

During the surge the opposition doesn't block your destiny, it propels you forward incredibly speedily.

Stay in faith and the storm is always followed by the surge--the difficulty pushes you forward, assured.

The more pulled back, the more you're shot forward. The more they block, the more you're honored.

KEY: Stay in faith while being pulled back. Keep a good attitude then the surge rewards in fact.

Don't be fooled--a surge is coming. Something is happening you can't see, then the exploding.

Nature indicates: That the storm is always followed by the surge of being propelled ahead, ok?

DECREASE IS A SIGN OF PROPULSION AHEAD SOON

The pulling back is temporary and the decrease is a sign you're about to go full throttle to destiny.

The enemy wouldn't be fighting you so hard if he wasn't aware of your amazing gifts unheard.

Talk like it's gonna happen, see it on the horizon: that's faith being released for success, son.

SUDDENLY...

After much opposition it finally happens SUDDENLY: favor, money, healing, public appreciation honey.

Discouraged and broke then ONE good break and you're back on your feet and loved by the folks.

Suddenly things went in my favor and the right people showed up: the light burst in non-stop.

God said "you've been pulled back long enough, it's time for your surge" and suddenly it all emerged.

He propelled me out of sickness to good health, from lack to abundance, injustice to leadership.

The bible's definition of "restoration": To receive back more than you lost and to start again.

The devil thought he won over me but actually he EQUIPPED me to help hurting people, see?

TERROR OF THE WORLDLY

Just like most I suffered heartbreak even terror over people and their cruelty--I became weak/skinny.

Voted the most likely to succeed, in this war I was beaten down/slandered and became weak-kneed.

It was like I had a bull's eye painted on me from birth, I was always in hot water and cursed.

In college I'd speak out and be bashed for it--I sought solace in alcohol and got smashed/lit.

I became a Christian conservative early and Jesus became real to me but isolation was a tragedy.

The anything-goes college atmosphere was dirty, debauched, silly, angry so that was my reality.

Despite liberal sisters image of "goodness" they were so callous/competitive it increased stress.

I loved the Lord and Jesus but when I joined a church it was social, requiring my presence.

I lost god consciousness in churches and wanted to stay home with the word, angels and holy spirit.

TROUBLES IN LIBERAL LAND

I dropped one relation after another, with the worldly I felt sullied/unhappy and just wanted my Father.

Men were out to use me, women to put down and compete with me--I had to face it constantly.

If you're different or can't/won't adapt to their crap you've had it cuz it's all conformity darnit.

Since feminism began, women were conformists to the absolute narrative by ostracizing dissidents.

Tho' this "absolute" narrative continually changes she will go along with it though it deranges.

I kept company with cats, dogs and God. I looked out the window and wrote though I'm flawed.

There are many like me who just can't relate to the social world of hugging/kissing and being unfree.

I went to A.A. meetings and say "so glad to be here tonight" and it was a lie, I was bored/no insight.

My ONLY solace was home and solitude when my whole world would open up, free of the rude.

As isolation and the "I" progressed, the world would argue against it and come over to confront/harass.

ESCAPE TO DESERT WILDERNESS

I escaped to the wilderness to be alone where I lived for 20+ years and God made Himself known.

Living as a desert recluse where I was happiest brought even more infamy with the clueless.

People always made me hopeless and unproductive, solitude gave me HOPE as a writer, prolific.

With a thirst for God [theist] I was only happy in His light and when lost, silly people were my boss.

I'd start looking up old friends on the internet and wasting time like that: people-worship crap.

If I had a couple drops of hope it helped me to get thru each day with active work not just mope.

Devil doesn't want us to have hope--he wants us hopeless. Put me with people, it's accomplished.

In solitude I had no homesickness or feeling of being disgraced/displaced but right at home, the Ace.

HOPE: SOMETHING GOOD'S ABOUT TO HAPPEN

Instead of "no one understands me" which they didn't, I couldn't care less cuz they're stupid.

Biblically, hope is a positive expectation that something good is about to happen--I had it.

I met husband in a dusty ghosttown--impossible! My life turned around overcoming all obstacles.

Then God got a hold of me thru some weird poetry and that's how I present this New Psychology.

Then one day God yanked me outa the wilderness cabin and put me in a safe state in a mansion.

How could this all happen in a lonely desert cabin? Well, when God's your Champion it's common.

RESTORATION IS THE WHOLE THING

God restored me tho' I made mistakes uncorrectable and messed up relationships forever too.

Scriptures say God gives us double for former trouble if we do things His way despite struggle.

All things work together for good for those who love God. After all this I'm sure of it and am awed.

God satisfies our years with good things so that our youth is restored like the eagles--we get wings.

Don't become discouraged or spiritless fearing the body is wasting for the inner is daily renewing.

Since we're daily renewing, "old" is an attitude not a number of years--at 90 you're a youthful seer.

Stop talking old ["everything's falling apart, it hurts, I can't do that I'm too old"] you faithless bore.

The more you talk "old" the older you look and the more other's agree with you--avoid this hook.

So we're all vanity--but a loving Father restores our youth! He knows we're vain, that is the truth.

A sour or give-up attitude will be instantly restored to a brand new one of hope--how divinely cool.

THE PIT VS. YOUR DREAMS

The "pit" is a necessary phase I guess, cure for the arrogant to become humble and God's very best.

You don't need a literary agent with God. Just make books available then one day they're all bought.

God doesn't abort dreams. He doesn't start a thing and not finish it, so unbury these please.

He wouldn't put the promise in your heart if He wasn't going to bring it to pass, so rejoice!

Though it didn't happen on your timetable so you buried it, it is still alive to God and His Spirit.

When God wakes up the dormant in you--the potential and talent--they'll all know in a moment.

DEALING WITH THE COMMUNIST SPIRIT

The globalists pay big bucks to journalists who influence millions--stands to reason, doesn't it?

Unbury whatever people talked you out of or all delays and disappointments that shut you up.

How do you dig it all up? Start talking like it's gonna happen, dust off those dreams and get goin'.

People will always put it down esp. if you're a writer. The devil doesn't want that book by a pro-lifer.

"You're too old"--but God said your latter days will be better than the former and your path brighter.

Unbury dreams: The bible says God's calling on our life is irrevocable--He doesn't change His mind.

Your time is coming: your mistakes didn't cancel your destiny no matter what you did honey.

Our great God knew every mistake we'd make, every person doing us wrong, every bad break.

It's the communist spirit: If you have more than them you DESERVE to be ripped off darnit.

The first time I met the woman she sized me up then slammed me on my back/showed who's one-up.

Women are cruel to each other and if you haven't noticed this you've become dense or callous.

You have ingroups and outgroups--insiders to the queen don't get attitude or behaviors so mean.

People crave to be the ingroup to avoid the punishments of being the outgroup but I refuse.

That's the human rat race man. It's chaos as your reality vacillates with the likes/dislikes of fans.

I'm filled with HOPE that something incredible is gonna happen at ANY moment, I can feel it!

ELIMINATING PEOPLE OBSTRUCTIONS

Eliminating people obstructions mostly was what brought this on: total world success/renowned.

Women are emotional so when they rule they let everything outa hell then confirm it as well.

There's nothing more vicious too since not tempered by centuries of honor and patience.

The world thinks it's men who are aggressive and rabid but have you ever witnessed her at it?

And when they get into power, watch out. A Maxine Watters or Nancy Pelosi: stiff-necked and wrong.

Women let it all outa hell then confirm it as well--that's "loving/forgiving" but I'm here to tell...

Stop saying I'm defined by my mistakes you ape.

OLD FREIGHT/DEAD WEIGHT

Gotta leave em all behind if you have to--not family/pets but those who block your future.

If they lied to you, robbed you, pulled a fast one, imposed on you--let em go and no more blue.

It's time for you to unload some dead weight, old freight. They don't fit where you're goin, ok?

Clean out every drawer and weed your friendship garden and you'll shoot ahead fast I reckon.

That's the way God is: promises we thought were dead God didn't despite our disappointments.

Despite mistakes He's still gonna promote you and take you where you could never go on your own.

What held us back? We quit believing--we let circumstances/bad breaks talk us out of it.

Most of the political correctness comes from a sick twisted view of Christianity--is it in your family?

This view says we should cut off ourselves to not be dominant as "fascists" and let the rest rise up.

Traitors don't believe in their birthright or power over Satan thru Christ, "it's all good" despite.

False Christians are smart but taken over by poli-correctitude demoting white men, screwed.

Feminism/globalism says "we're gonna take control of the men and make em weak for their own good".

Feminists are willing to bring down our culture and society cuz they can't beat men any other way.

POSTMODERN STUNTS

How to get a lot of work done: declare a vacation, then creativity erupts and it's finished in elation.

Yes we have free will but God still knows what we're gonna do cuza His omniscience--future too.

Colleges jack up prices, decrease quality, push identity politics and Marxism, postmodern stunts.

It's the social sciences and humanities most affected but now even physics and astronomy is tainted.

The worst is their view of history as the domination of a tyrannical male patriarchy: this is false.

You keep giving a little of yourself away until pretty soon you have no power/don't know who you are.

They assume COMPETENCE is the same as tyranny over us and thus they attack those who are best.

Magan Rapinoe says dumb things on a regular basis but it's all-ok cuz she's accepted: leftist/feminist.

Dont let em use subtle conversational tricks to bully you into looking dumb. Study Jordan Peterson

He starts with "so you're saying" then proceeds to oversimplify or mischaracterize what I said.

SYSTEM COOLING IS PALPABLE

Trust your instincts about people--not paranoid, if you sense a distinct cooling it's probably true.

I can speak to one person and know about the whole system. If there's a cooling, they've been talkin'

You know the gossip grapevine so when you sense it remove yourself from it for a fresh start honey.

Lowminds will always judge highminds and that's the persecution you avoid by choosing high.

Wait for the few who appreciate your genius and while doing your work stay free from the rest.

If smart you'll move out with the country bumpkins but that's a whole new lesson I reckon.

You're smart/educated, they're not [tho' they work good] so how to avoid the communist spirit?

The lowminds murmur, resent you, envy you, and when allowed around your stuff will rob you.

They naturally think: "they have all that and I have so little so it's a good thing to rob these peeps."

They naturally think: "they have all that and I have so little so it's a good thing to rob and belittle."

THE WICKED ARE LIKE CHAFF

The wicked are like chaff--worthless, dead, without substance--which the wind drives away.

The way of the ungodly [living outside God's will] shall perish: end in ruin and come to nought.

The minute you show a weakness they gather together seeking to cast your control asunder.

You've only tried to help em but they sense your loftiness so at these times can get violent.

The wonderful Lord laughs and has them in derision and in supreme contempt--He mocks them.

My Father speaks to them in His deep anger and troubles, terrifies, confounds them in His fury.

I will declare the decree of the Lord: He said to me, you are my son: this day I have begotten you.

He said: Ask of Me and I will give you the nations as your inheritance--and I felt secure ever since.

And the persecutors? "You shall break them with a rod of iron: You shall dash em in pieces".

Serve with reverential awe/worshipful fear, rejoicing in high spirits in trembling lest you displease Him.

Kiss the Son [pay homage in purity] lest He be angry and you perish in the way. Psalms 2: 12

Be PURE for soon is His wrath kindled. Reverential fear and awe means you're joyful but tremble.

Blessed [happy, fortunate, and TO BE ENVIED] are all those who seek refuge and put their trust in Him!

Arizona Strip is like living in a painting. esp. Cane Beds: crickets at night/crows in the morning.

PSALMS SAVED ME IN THE WILDERNESS

Lord, how they are increased that trouble me! Many rise up against me in insults, slanders, robberies.

The stiff-necked are obviously slandering me behind my back so I'll turn inside and pray to my Dad.

They say there's no hope for me in God but He was a shield for me and lifted my head instead.

I will not be afraid of 10,000 people siding against the Chic for God'll strike ALL foes on the cheek.

God promised He'd break the teeth of the ungodly, and when I saw Jim again he looked like a hillbilly.

Churches have fallen wherever women rule em cuz they allow evil to blossom/refuse to judge em.

Fake Christian women end up with little criminals surrounding em cuz they're so forgiving/loving.

They hurt me so much, I don't need to put my finger on it--it's ineffable but to me obvious as hell.

I trust my instincts and felt like I walked into a den of demons and disarray, I felt hated and betrayed.

I'm not gonna feel sorry for the Jezebel like I always do and get re-enmeshed in that sorry stew.

FAKE CHRISTIAN WOMEN

They think they're good Christians tolerating that stuff but actually the spirit's gone, it's all bluff.

Women condone sin to be tolerant then sink in their own swill from a den of demons set to kill.

If you're a genius you gotta have the right comportment in a world of lowminded demons.

Lead me in Your right way because of my enemies for there is nothing trustworthy in them.

Their heart is destruction [a yawning gulf]...they flatter and make smooth with their tongue.

Hold them guilty, oh Lord! Let em fall by their own designs and counsels: cast em out due to sins.

Let us who put our trust in You shout for joy knowing You will defend us and thus have high spirits.

GOOD, EVIL AND CIVILIZED

I knew about good and evil but because back then people were more civilized you couldn't see it.

Of course there was always evil but it wasn't so "out there" and we didn't really see it--we were happier.

One reason "nothing is happening" is cuz you can't go back and the future isn't here yet, so persist.

The fact that it seems like nothing's happening is a sign it's about to explode like the Tsunamis.

Of course it's discouraging as hell--that's a sign you're the greatest, historically it's a symbol.

Of course nothing's happening--you're that unique. It's lonely at the top of a famous mountain peak.

If it's your destiny to be famous that'll be how you find yourself and you won't stop, it's all God.

I am ever-waiting for link to put it all together. I have HOPE: expecting good to happen for the clever.

What if you found out all that back pain was from someone you're still mad at? Forgive em hon'

Climate change is a UN-led ruse to establish a new world order and kids are the pawns/martyrs.

LIMBO requires faith: You're so progressed you can't go back and the future isn't here yet.

FAVOR MAKES YOU LIMITLESS

Thank God when FAVOR endorses you, brings you into prominence and takes you to new levels.

FAVOR keeps enemies from defeating me, favor makes me attractive, favor brings opportunity.

Favor causes us to excel: surely goodness and mercy follows me all of my life and all is well.

When you're in favor with God even a giant ten times your size can't defeat you, God's kid and prize.

You're not ignored you're HIDDEN under God's hand until that moment comes so prepare for it man.

Why not? If it feels good do it. There are apparently NO LINES or limits whatsoever with whomever.

Takes your eyes off of EVERYBODY and put em on your own inner reality THEN you'll be ready.

You're encouraging him to get dirtier and more outlandish until he eventually hits bottom on it inevitably

THE SHALLOW ARE UNFAITHFUL

They are shallow and say it's ok to be unfaithful. They give gays a bad name, or is it typical?

She didn't exactly sell me but gave him access and put me in harm's way with no accountability.

I don't feel a victim of my life. Had I had it any easier would I have the courage to overcome such strife?

The crowd of sorrows in your early life is preparing you for tomorrow which will be free of this strife.

It may not bother you but gross DISORDER bothers me because heaven is orderly.

I thank God every day that I'm so far away you can't bother me anymore and that's all I gotta say.

Here you thought certainly they appreciated you now to find out they're in a fog/haven't a clue.

My eye grew dim from grief, getting old due to all my enemies. Depart from me you workers of iniquity.

THE **LORD** IS MY CHAMPION AND SHIELD

The Lord has heard all my weeping and He cares. "God'll get em" is my slogan re: the tares.

Let all my enemies be ashamed/sorely troubled, let em turn back and be put to shame suddenly.

Though I may hate her guts [for good reason] she'll never know it, at our last meeting I gave her gifts.

I dropped one association after another lest I be morally offended: William James on the saints.

In God I take refuge/put my trust for He saved me from my persecutors and He delivered me.

I thank my enemies for triggering in me the power to overcome them through a success surge.

They trampled my soul to the ground/lay my honor in the dust but God swooped in, a divine bust.

My sin was this: that I looked for pleasure, beauty and truth in human creatures not in Him.

This search in myself and other creatures led to pain, confusion and error: carnal terror.

The ex-gay said he "just knew" being with another man could never be glorifying to God, whew.

NARROW GATE: FEW FRIENDS

Enter by the narrow gate for the gate is wide and the way is easy that leads to destruction. Mathew

Those entering the wide gate are many for the gate is narrow/way is hard that leads to life, few find it.

The climate-alarmist media environment is bringing on the new psychological affliction "eco anxiety".

When my enemies turned back they stumbled and perished before you. Psalms 9: 3

Lift Yourself against the rage of my enemies and stir up justice and vindication You've commanded.

Against "child separation" but ok with infanticide-- contradictions are ridiculous when IQ is diminished.

You have rebuked nations/destroyed the wicked and have blotted out their name forever and ever.

You have plucked up and overthrown their cities: the very memory of them has vanished.

The Lord will also be a refuge and high tower for the oppressed in times of trouble and desperation.

THE TABLES HAVE TURNED, IT'S THE LORD

The tables have turned: what was on top is now on the bottom and the bottom the top, I'm stoked.

Why would God help you if you don't care about Him or even seek after Him? Your helper is Satan.

He who avenges injustice remembers us, He does not forget the cry of the afflicted/poor/humble.

Have mercy upon me Lord: consider how I am afflicted by those who hate me. Psalms 9: 13

That I may shout to the world and tell EVERYONE about all your praises! Lord, please raise me.

The nations have sunk down in the pit they made, in their hidden net their own foot is caught.

Make Yourself known! Execute judgment so the wicked are ensnared in work of their own hands.

The wicked shall be turned back headlong into premature death with all those forgetting God.

CULTURAL PSYCHOLOGICAL CRISES

I'm not a sadistic leftist scientist it's about true reality and our present psychological crises.

God is leading me, I can feel it! I prayed for guidance feeling empty but now it's the Spirit.

The needy shall not always be forgotten! Your hopes and expectations shall not perish forever!

ARISE, Oh Lord! Let not man prevail! Let the nations be judged before You. Psalm 9: 19.

Put them in fear, realizing their frail nature. Make the nations know they are but men = dustbins.

OUR FOES AS CHAMPIONS

Wicked in pride/arrogance pursue and persecute the poor: let em be taken by their own schemes.

For the wicked boasts/sings the praises of his own heart's desire and the greedy despises the Lord.

Wicked in pride will **NOT** seek, inquire for or yearn for God: he thinks there is no God who punishes.

your judgements are far above and out of his sight so he never thinks of em and just sneers at his foes.

The wicked man thinks in his heart: I shall not be moved and will never come to want or adversity.

The wicked's mouth is full of cursing, deceit, oppression, fraud, trouble, mischief and sin.

The wicked slays the innocent. He watches stealthily for the poor [the helpless and unfortunate].

SAVING PSALMS IN MEMORY

He lurks in secret places like a lion in his thicket that he may seize the poor and draw him into his net.

SHOCK is when it happens by a friend you trusted. A sudden change in your life like being busted.

Foe thinks: God has forgotten, He has hidden His face, He will never see my deed--wait and see!

Arise, O Lord! Lift up Your hand: forget not the humble [the very patient and crushed].

Why does the wicked man renounce God? What makes him think God won't call to account?

You've seen it, yes! You note trouble and grief to requite it with Your hand, Helper of the fatherless.

Why would God support you if you never seek after Him and even spurn Him? He won't and me neither.

The unfortunate commits himself to you: You are the helper of the fatherless--break arm of the wicked.

The Lord is King forever and ever, the nations will perish out of His hand. My favorite verse.

Oh Lord: You have now heard the longing and urgent desires of the humble and oppressed: success!

You will now prepare, strengthen and direct their hearts. You will cause Your ear to hear.

To do justice to the fatherless and oppressed, so that man may not terrify them any more. Psalm 10: 18

REVELATIONS ABOUT FOOD

You say you're thin/healthy, let's see if that's true: Pull up your shirt, see the rolls/face the truth.

I implored him: please don't bring ice cream into the house cuz when I start I can't stop myself.

Nut-butters aren't the best but are ok/harmless. But ice cream is a chemical mess not dairy goodness.

I wouldn't give ice cream to your dogs, tho' they love it and crave it too--these chemicals can kill you.

Bakery: the problem isn't the flour, butter and sugar but all the chemicals that go into it for sure.

ice cream isn't "dairy goodness" but rather frozen chemicals sequestered into ROLLS OF FAT.

The carnivore diet cures acid reflux? My acid group couldn't believe this, it goes against the books.

It's the American breakfast: bacon and eggs. Many people live on it only and they are strong--ya dig?

With carbs you gotta keep eating all day, they trigger hunger and you're not getting anywhere, ok?

Reaction to nightshades [potatoes, tomatoes, peppers, eggplant, blueberries]? Acid reflux like everything else.

I want transformational healing and if I'm a carnivore to do it so be it--acid reflux is the main thing.

If I didn't take smoothies I wouldn't eat, other than cherry tomatoes, grapes, bacon, a little cheese.

We're told to eat green veggies but what of the lectins, goitrogens, oxalates-- poison, all of it.

I don't need to go to a gym. Just by a busy life and doing house and yard work I stay fit and thin.

I just don't like the carnivore diet. I crave fruit smoothies to soothe esophagus but I'll try it.

Fruit smoothies, grapes, cherry tomatoes, piece cheese equals no acid reflux or a sneeze.

We have the American breakfast [bacon and eggs] then in the afternoon we have a few grapes.

THE AMERICAN BREAKFAST

No matter how hungry animal fat satiates then we reverse matrices later with the cleansing grapes.

I was a little concerned when Ray dropped 50 pounds but he was young again not old/round.

At first he was skinny fat, living on cookies/this and that but with animal fat, he's now cut/a cute chap.

He is SO appreciative that I have his breakfast ready and he feels so good throughout the day.

Make use of modern science. For example I can have bacon but eggs are non-immune protocol.

Eat bacon feel pretty good all day, eat eggs and I have acid reflux, dizziness and wanna die.

The autoimmune protocol says no nuts or seeds. Try it, maybe you can have one of these things.

But if you're eating a bunch of nutbutter and have acid reflux later, I'd note the AIP on the matter.

Are you sick today because of the soy- and corn syrup-filled "protein bar" you had yesterday?

EARLY NIGHTS AND PERFECTING SKILLS

God has blessed you in the work of your hands. He knows you're trudging through this great wilderness.

Forty years of trudging was the Israelites. I can relate to that but eventually you're released.

I am beseeching you Lord, based on your Words, to make it all come to pass, what I've requested.

Your words above Lord: I've told the world what you said and will tell em what You did till I'm dead.

Please don't let em win Lord. They don't care about you, I worship you daily/every minute in the word.

I'm going by what you said Lord, not being selfish. I'm standing on your every word which I relish.

I'll shout to the world what a great God you are, coming through for me in this terrible war.

My whole life is about putting puzzles together and the Creative Act too as I'm completing her.

BOLDLY TELL THE TRUTH NOW

It's a wicked war of realities and they are vanity, rivalries, debaucheries, treacheries, robberies.

All behind a nice face. As women take over we see fallen churches who don't know true scripture.

I can't stand em either Father, I'm ashamed what they've become and find them shallow and dumb.

But now, don't forget my dreams which You anointed before my birth. I'm ready, please don't tarry.

Women are sure they're right forgiving everything without repentance, creating criminals/dunces.

I'll show the world how You're right and they're wrong every day I live. I'll explain/debunk contradictions.

You said You'd make me the head and not the tail. I've waited and worked all my life to no avail.

That's all I gotta say, You've heard my prayer and I won't detain You but will wait for You every minute.

GOD NEEDS NO LITERARY AGENTS

A writer should self-publish NOT wait for an agent to accept it until life's end--get it out there friend.

Don't give up: 40% of big-sellers last year started as self-published before an agent picked them up!

Let no agent tell you nothing happens by self-publishing--just market to the nitch today.

Agents are just realizing that authors don't need them and it scares them--they're right, they are useless man.

When you get exhausted from agent rejections filling your inbox, take matters in your own hands fast.

Lit Agents now: Is there any chance you might love my book, represent me and get me a book deal? A: No.

Agents make fun of authors, they disdain them. They're quick with rejections but God'll listen to you man.

You don't need these creepy middlemen--dinosaurs from a previous era that's dying--no more need for em.

Agents don't know you or your work, they feel superior--just want money from mediocrity and many are jerks.

What sells your book WITHOUT an agent is FAME. That's all you need then publishers come around again.

I just wanted to get my work out there and whether it sold or not was irrelevant tho' I knew it was clever.

I decided I would never again seek an agent--after decades of work, an added torture. God would decide my future.

And if nothing happens, so what? I learned so much from writing all this maybe that's all Father God wanted.

Stop seeking creepy middlemen ["literary agents"]. You're a child of God—He picks the best for His charges.

WOLVES IN SHEEP'S CLOTHING

The "Christian" literary agents are the worst since they're rejecting what doesn't fit their narrow view first.

Many Christian "conservatives" are total liberals in their views. We need Civics so the dumb can break thru.

Christian "conservatives" often sound like anti-Trumpers: they agree to impeachment/want open borders.

Don't trust em because they're labeled "Christian" cuz heresies abound and they're a foe/not a friend.

There are Christians who voted for Hillary Clinton tho' a villain and those lovin' migrants tho' they be killin'

The churches help illegals get into our country. This is Christianity? No, it's women running things.

Mass illegal immigration is an armed invasion and churches falling for it are always based on false doctrine.

It's an armed invasion without guns--by a different worldview altogether throwing citizens asunder.

The army is the invaders, educated to hate us before they come in with Soros-funded debit cards.

The border issue proves churches have fallen into feminist psychology and their love of paganism.

The fallen church revs up membership by cute little skits that go against the gospel which is absurd to twits.

They demand you forgive anything and everything never taking a stand against immorality--it's not Christianity.

In the false church one gets embroiled In politix, klatches, group tyranny, jealousies and Jezebel splits.

In the false church the Big Act takes dominance and that's why everything becomes virtue-signaling.

HIGH ORDER/BORDERS EQUALS DISGUST

I had nothing but problems, born in hot water. Up and down, highs and lows, helter skelter.

No one imposed order on my life, I had to learn that on my own. More orderly, higher boundaries.

HIGH order plus HIGH boundaries equals DISGUST. I love that, it's a perfect description of the situation.

Order came into thought life too. It was a formula: all disease is obstruction, true friends are few.

Human involvements brought downturns. As I took on their reality about me, I'd conform by lunacy.

I saw how order made me happy and creative but arising early was the most evocative.

When the herd's asleep I get inspired. I start my day before midnight and can't wait to get started.

This is entirely unique having evolved thru a life and copy if you want you will just fruitlessly strive.

So getting up early plus emaculate order = success but only after eliminating the people mess.

CREATIVITY NEEDS MATURITY

Early life: perfecting skills and overcoming obstacles builds muscle so creative spirit comes through.

Creativity with immaturity goes wrong--need both: perfecting skills and multi-adaptation [maturation].

When I didn't get my early nights I was unhappy and groggy and when people brought disorder, angry.

Catnaps when needed, that's the way to do it. Nights are MOST inspiring then sleep on tables.

I can see how my whole entire life evolved to this point. In fact I mine it for gems as I think.

Some people go into military or jail to mature, I lived alone in a desert cabin in solitude on 1000 acres.

Living in the world of a small liberal town made me so crazy until I realized it was them not me.

When people are distracted by sins, desires and scams they make big mistakes man so I say BAN.

The saints can become tortured by conscience but God can erase all this after their repentance.

OVERCOMING LIBERAL INFLUENCES

It was sickening to be around em: a callous world where there is no justice and it's ok for vices.

Pagan influences are there lest one actively rejects them. The feminists love em, it's astonishin'

These people have no lines and it's all about sex. They may get violent too, they're under a hex.

Sheltered, I had no idea what people were like. Finding out was my Ph.D. in the streets--yikes!

When I saw they were without lines I became terrified of my guests and that was the beginning I guess.

I have strict lines/regal order, they're what bedlam must mean, it was terrible/makes me shudder.

When you're hanging with them it's judgment from an inferior entity, it's in words/gestures honey.

AVOID: She gossips constantly and is a very poor housekeeper, not-quite-clean, trashy disorder.

I knew who he was when he said "I'm not adopted" in front of his adopted brothers, like he was one-up.

RETURN TO FIRST NATURE

A writer writes because he writes. Indeed he cannot NOT write since resolving contradiction removes strife.

Tho' raped 200 times by age ten, I still wouldn't change anything from all the benefits. Joyce Meyer

Why was he healed? He made the SWITCH between "IF it be Your will" to "Lord I know it IS your will"!

Us Christian conservatives were pushed around for years: mocked, ruined and degraded by peers.

Buddy you're two inches from having to walk the plant due to your arrogance, it's God's promise.

They've been in power for 70 years and they can't believe their cool music's not playin' no more.

They looked so cool and they made the big money so there was no way we could achieve victory.

When their balloon popped in 2016 they were petulant children unable to accept the new scene.

We weren't stupid, we were asleep. Illegal immigrant floods were what woke me up to globalist creeps.

We all have lucid memories of snobbish sisters and friends inculcating these narrative and trends.

They acted so superior since the seventies. It was self-evident to them, tautologies of the friendlies.

"What smart person would believe in the bible?" my Ph.D. sponsor said--it was so hard to get ahead.

Kenya West Phenomenon may be key to restoration along with the military--not the courts etc.

You should be afraid of only one thing: that is GOD. Because He controls everything. Kanye West

LAND WITHOUT JUSTICE

The liberal world of hyper-forgiveness is actually a land without justice and it creates criminals.

We're all waiting for something, it's the whole thing as God watches HOW we wait--do we stay in faith?

We've concentrated on rights and privileges but not responsibility and meaning for 50 years.

By taking responsibility I ORDER my life and that brings meaning--a real cornucopia feeling.

People are now shallow with impulsive pleasures and then storms wreck them. Jordan Peterson

Get outa the left brain--sometimes it's more fruitful to muse and dream like a child on vacation, see?

Somehow I feel destiny. I hear trucks on a highway and it reminds me of something/Lord fill me.

When I was broke and down you told the "dumb bigot" to go away. Now that I'm rich you're back, but hey...

Crows in the morning, afternoon breeze, crickets at night and the cows walk by: my NEW LIFE

KAREN KELLOCK 103

A new theory in social psychology: the tyranny of groups vs. the individual in unique presentation. Collective insanity, the contagion of lunacy. What does it take to be a champion standing out in a sea of sharks? That is the essence of the writings of Karen Kellock. Koestler [1962] has noted the blending of art and science marks all discoveries. "She is a maestro with words, all about the herds." Mansell Pattison, Postdoctoral Chair, UCI School of Medicine.

KAREN KELLOCK 103
Author's Notes '23

NO MAN KNOWS OUR HISTORY
NO WORRIES, IT'S OVER FOR GOOD
STOP STUFFING FROM OUTSIDE
FAMING: MASS ATTRACTIONS
GET READY FOR ORATION
DANGEROUS SOY INVASION
WHERE ARE AMERICAN BAKERS
FAMILY, FAITH AND FREEDOM

KAREN KELLOCK 103
Author's Notes '23

NO MAN KNOWS OUR HISTORY

The Superior Man said: "no man knows my history." This comes from logic and Einstein theory.

Lib land: Since gossip was their major weapon they incited riots against me from other humans.

The more I suffered over invasion the bigger/tougher the defenses I built up in compensation.

The fastest way to build boundaries is to trap yourself with a gang of undisciplined greedy boys.

The fastest way to build boundaries is to trap yourself with a buncha mean girls filled with envy.

It doesn't take long for losers in a small liberal town to peg/put you down and spread it all around.

You're encouraged on the way up but with success many drop off as past supports dissolve.

She had legal power over me and she was a bully. A big black cloud of put downs from jealousy.

It's easier to forgive once you accept the FACT it's the only way to get rid of em in your spirit.

I forgive you because that puts me in eternity. If I hold a grudge you're inside of me, blocking.

Author's Notes 2023

NO WORRIES, IT'S OVER FOR GOOD

That sort of thing would never happen again so there's no reason to think of it again, just the lesson.

As a sinner you were lonely and bored so you actually wanted their company: relieving words.

Don't recall the abrasion just the lesson so that situation would never be happening again.

It's a long journey, the hero's path--treasure hard to attain, philosopher's stone--then complete it.

The most important thing to do take a toke put music on and look out the window, forget videos.

STOP STUFFING FROM OUTSIDE

Stop stuffing from the outside. It's your inner fidelity to take it all in we wanna increase, aye.

They make sex common as going to the bathroom. It's disgusting--keep it sacred. Kellock, Marion

Of children trapped at home with mothers some suffered more than others or it was over.

A mischief maker, an untruthteller, the real devil in the family. Queen Victoria on her daughter.

You've given birth to the Creative Act, it's just a matter of when they'll pick up on it/it'll be a smash.

Without self-control someone else will take control and you could be trapped for life ya know.

It sticks with you having your face pushed in the mud. It's humiliating but who avenges it? God.

Author's Notes 2023

It's a giant joke when you're whole bad past is wiped out. It's God's black out too, He said it, oh!

FAMING: MASS ATTRACTIONS
Better Repent!

It's a matter of God's timing. A moment comes of mass attractions to the true self called faming.

Don't fear being seen cuz it's worse being unseen like a cog in the wheel/sand on the beach see.

To be revealed on that level requires purity or bring yourself down thru slips/faux paux see.

For every sin there's a compensation in the present. Better get pure before speaking: REPENT.

There comes a moment where you MUST do it. Don't worry, like before it's over before you know it.

GET READY FOR ORATION

Are you destined to. be a speaker, an orator? Then you MUST do it, face your fears, or disappear.

Enantiodromia: face your fears and do it or die in the gutter outa frustration you didn't live it.

To pet cat on lap gotta have rigid control of diet, that's all there is to it: TOTAL LOAD explains it.

It was like being in a prison: we're all a mere number and it's mutual abusin' with no escapin'.

Remove the soul tie from your eyes and he's not such a handsome guy. Satan's clever that way. aye.

Mourn past support dissolution then go forward to all God has for you. Recall life is short too.

Author's Notes 2023

Where are your detractors, ridiculers and mockers now? Dead or gone, disempowered mean gals.

When a female genius arrives at success she's so exhausted she can't enjoy it. Simone de Bouvier

DANGEROUS SOY INVASION

It tastes just like caramel and nuts but it gave me a headache and the afternoon was acidic.

European bakers didn't give in to soy so the people don't show disastrous effects like us see.

Soy is used in all bakeries and it's been that way for decades. Look up Dangers of Soy ok.

What IS human ugliness? Protuberances, puffiness, lopsidedness, bloated lower end, opaqueness.

It used to be cookies, candies and pastries were healthy, made with natural ingredients.

Would you like to live on cookies, candies and pastries? Just make em yourself and it's all healthy.

Natural goody ingredients: maple syrup, honey, nuts, seeds, butter, flour, fruits, coconut.

Yes we want the donuts and morning pastries but not this way honey: soy makes ya' ugly.

WHERE ARE AMERICAN BAKERS

Where are American bakers who don't use soy and say it? I can't find one, it's a cultural kill fest.

Bakery is: flour, sugar, sweeteners, nuts, seeds, fruits and other natural ingredients. NOT soy sis.

Author's Notes 2023

They actually say soy is better protein enrichment. I'm telling you folks on looks it's a bagashit.

Breakfast is the most important or only meal to the Scotch so I say: get a non-soy bakery.

Cherished bakeries switching to soy and not telling the folks. This is a mean trick/let em know.

See how quickly nine pounds of water retention goes out thru a short fast. Learn, experience.

You ate two candy bars made of soy/etc. and the body bloated up with water to act as a buffer.

Candy actually used to be good for you. A licorice, a chocolate covered nut, even caramel if true.

When God says to fast, you fast and you don't go back. Resolve, fidelity to a vow, that's muscle.

See the difference between shortbread [flour sugar butter] and adulterated/poisoned others.

You eat shortbread you're better off for it. You eat a milky way or almond joy and you're SICK.

Delicious caramel used to be butter and sugar melted. Now its chemicals but you can't tell.

FAMILY, FAITH AND FREEDOM

Faith, family and freedom: that's the conservative. Rinos blocking our direction are the problem.

Hitler became popular when he called them superior with blamed/labeled groups as obstructors.

I'm done, let's have a party lasting forever. It deserves recognition and remuneration for clever.

Author's Notes 2023

I start my weekends on Wednesday then by time Saturday's here I'm well into the party.

Friends fall away/die one by one so you don't feel it til the end: they're gone/you're alone but God..

Creativity: I've had dry periods [but always something going on inside of me] and spurts of activity.

I don't make things happen. I make myself apt to receive it when God lays out His plan.

KAREN KELLOCK

103

KAREN KELLOCK 103

YOU WERE MY PH.D. IN THE STREETS
OPEN SEASON ON WHITE PEOPLE NOW
ENERGY WASTE OF SENSITIVES
BITTERNESS/ANGER ARE CONTAMINATES/DRAIN
GENIUS CANNOT FIT
PROTECT YOURSELF AS IF FAMOUS
GOD IS JUSTICE, SO RELAX!
ALONE, NEVER LONELY OR BORED
PATIENCE: IT ALL HAPPENS IN A SEQUENCE
HIX POLITIX
ALONE AT HOME I SOAR
NOTHING WORSE THAN A MULTICULTURALIST
DEEP EMPATHS AND RIDICULE
PROFESSIONAL SHOW-OFFS/PUTDOWN ARTISTS
JEZEBEL TAKES OFFENSE BEING DENSE
SO SICK OF THE LOW CLASS MASS ASS
JEZEBEL IS VILE AND VICIOUS
WHITE PEOPLE REPLACEMENT
INVASION WITHOUT ANY DEFENSE
YES WE CAN JUDGE, AND SHOULD
GUILTY CONSCIENCE IS LOST BOLDNESS
THE WAITING PHASE IS A TEST
EVERYONE'S BAD, NO ONE GOOD
THE TRUTH HURTS SO IS BESMERCHED
GOD GIVES EM UP TO DEGRADING PASSIONS
WOMEN CAVE IN LAST
A DEPRAVED MIND GETS KOOKY IDEAS
KILLED BY OUR LIE FORTRESS

KAREN KELLOCK 103

WOMEN: IT'S NOT REALLY HER
DAD IS DEMONIZED
A FALLEN NATURE SEEKS TO CONTROL
WHEN WOMEN RULE THERE IS CHAOS
REBELLIOUS FEMALE PREACHERS
MUST SEE THRU TV HERESIES: WORD AND FAITH
SOFTENING OF SIN HERESY
THEY DARKEN GOD'S. COUNSEL WITH ADD-ONS
GOD GIVES THE ONLY CHANGE IN YOU
STOP COMPLAINING ABOUT PEST CONTROL LESSONS
SEE THE PAST AS A LESSON ONLY
FROM TOTAL VICTIM TO BOOK DATA
NEW DEMOCRACY RUN BY MEDIA
BEWITCHING LIE: NEED WORKS
BEWITCHED: THE CROSS IS NOT ENOUGH?
THE CROSS SETTLES IT ALL
WORKS SEVERS US FROM CHRIST
BOUNDARIES AND BORDER CONTROL
ALCOHOL THE MORAL DISINHIBITOR
IMPOSED ON BY PREVIOUS SYSTEMS
BLOOD-WASHED MEMORY
IT'S WHAT I DO.
JEZEBEL AIN'T SPIRITUAL SHE'S SOCIAL
ONE.EVENT CHANGES LIFE FOREVER
THE LESSONS WERE HARD BUT FORGET EM NOW
CHANGED DEMOGRAPHY: NOT SO BIG YOU SEE
THEY CONSIDER THEMSELVES GODS
IS HER SILENCE A RUDDER TO CONTROL?

KAREN KELLOCK 103

WOMEN: THE CHURCHES HAVE FALLEN
SICK SEEKER-SENSITIVE MOVEMENT
NEW CHURCH EAR-TICKLERS AND SOCIALS
SHEEP'S CLOTHES ARE WHITE
THE MOST WORTHWHILE PAST TIME
PURE DOCTRINE IS SIMPLE
LIGHT TO GUIDE OR BRICK TO CARRY?
ABSTAIN MEANS COMPLETE
PERVERSIONS OF TRUTH IS MOST WICKED
SEXUAL IMMORALITY IS WORST
INVASIONS OF THE FALSE CHURCH
MUST HAVE DOCTRINAL CLARITY/CONVICTION
DEVELOP THE ANTITHETICAL MENTALITY
BLURRED LINES IS THE FEMINIZATION OF THE CHURCH
WORLDLY CHATTER AND UNGODLINESS
SEEK KNOWLEDGE LIKE HIDDEN TREASURE
WAY TO HEAVEN IS APART FROM THE CROWD
SHALLOW GOSPEL GOES TO HELL
SHALLOW AFFIRMATIONS
KAREN'S HEALTHY CANDIES
CANDY HEALERS
NUTS, COCONUT, FRUIT, SUPERFOODS, CACAO
CANDY IS A GOOD THING AGAIN
COLON CLEANSING CANDY
MEAL REPLACEMENT PAR EXCELLENCE
DESSERTS SPELLED BACKWARDS: STRESSED
ACID REFLUX IS KARMA FOR EARLY ERROR
FAST TO BALANCE TOTAL LOAD

You wouldn't be where you are without having started out with that arrogant entitled mentality, so forget it.

Who bashed you? Old crones inwardly jealous and downright pugnacious once getting the upper hand.

How did they get the upper hand? Your sins kept you down and shame enabled the Fallen Hero Syndrome.

If I didn't speak/write about this it would mean I went thru it all for nothing: people problems/system theory.

TRASHED BY SINNERS

Who trashed you? Old crones STEEPED in sin but socially approved so they can all side against you.

They don't know a thing about politics so they should just shut up but arrogance makes em mean and loud.

Your sins stood out like a sore thumb but theirs are socially approved so no big thing--now that's plain dumb.

We live in an ever-changing universe. Seasons change, tides rise and fall--success will come after all.

Refuse to adapt to what they think. As you mature you'll see it's all rinky-dink and that conformists stink.

If something is way wrong like this you gotta read the signs. You'd be way better off without him.

With memories you can't forget it is impossible to turn the page. Bring em up, blunt em: now go your way.

Life is a pie and sensitive deep-thinkers want more time for what fulfills them--it's not an insult just a rare find.

They felt insulted I'd rather stay home with a book than twiddle thumbs at a boring klatch so silly and dumb.

Being a sensitive is a good thing but in the world brings very low self-esteem cuz you're not on the team.

The best way to get boatloads of compassion is to go through stuff yourself. Joyce Meyer

Understanding your high sensitivity is crucial to seeing yourself and your needs as normal and valid, see?

Your feelings/needs/wants matter as much as anyone else's so voice them clearly [e.g. solitude] or draw boundaries.

When you treat yourself as if you matter others SEE and respond differently to your emotions and needs.

I overcame so many obstacles with so much pain in my life that my intense emotions were channeled into poetry.

I developed the skills like writing and vocabulary so that my RAW INSTINCT could come through beautifully.

The pianist or singer learns the skills so that the RAW INSTINCT can come thru/smoothed out/complete.

YOU DON'T HAVE TO SEE ANYONE

We don't want em coming over here with their rude ageist comments or officious questions--it's our HOME dear.

As long as its just US it's heaven on earth and we're joyfully creative all day putting things into proper place.

Highly sensitive people have an immense capacity for empathy but burnout when absorbing emotions.

We walk into a room and instantly sense the tension or joy--we are master non-verbal communicators.

We can "sense" emotion before it comes--and thus we hate conflict and can easily sense it is coming.

These emotions are not separate from us--to enter even a slightly tense atmosphere we feel tense themselves

Others can pick up on emotions but for us it's far more intense--during my bad eras I was with lunatics.

As a result we feel sad, irritable or lethargic--from absorbing emotion or yesterday being affected.

We can sense conflict is coming because we process info deeper and see the [patterned] cues/triggers quicker.

A RAISED EYEBROW, A NON-RESPONSE

A raised eyebrow, a non-response all means something to us--whereas others are completely/utterly dense.

Hypersensitives shun social as a loud aggravating siren of nobodies snubbing and sizing em up and down.

It's not that I don't like you, it's just that there are millions of fulfilling things I strive to do every moment too.

When I feel sad, irritable or lethargic I know I've taken someone else's burden on--I've done it again.

I've been eclipsed by another human being, I've lost parts of myself, I've been overridden or replaced--that's all.

My new life began when I started to PRIORITIZE [by knowing myself] and then set firm BOUNDARIES.

When someone's in my life I'm thinking about em all the time. If they're rotten or apathetic, how's my mind?

A sensitive must guard the mind--what get's in, who he is around--cuz he takes it all on and gets easily down.

With sustained conflict I get used to elevated stress levels until my crash: the hedge is down, in comes the devil.

I actually got used to living in exhaustion and anxiety for years. I became depleted, unrecognizable to peers.

I lost healthy glow, my skin just hung ya know--the stress of living in conflict/chaos is inconceivable to y'all.

INNER AND OUTER CIRCLES

In social eras where "being social" supersedes independence, sensitives are attacked for "rudeness".

Accepting rights to boundaries, listening to my body and taking a day off is how I am sustained as a sensitive.

Quietly observing and accepting what people are like is the boundary-setter, you just realize it and act smarter.

An inner circle of those you trust--subject to change--and an outer circle you treat with aristocratic reserve.

If someone's on your shit list you don't go back without thinking about it. You make FIRM decisions/reject.

As long as you have the devil inside they will hate you. Stop thinking thru a persecution complex, be true.

I always had ALL this in me--but before I knew it my brain was anarchy with all these concepts unfolding.

Whenever I feel drained, senseless or sad I know there's some cruel competition blocking energy fast.

Sterile hierarchies: that's what I sensed all around, like the sorority which I escaped early. Reject for clarity.

If they use too many words they aren't true intellectuals for the latter strive for meaning/understanding as primal.

Before one has self-control he has no self-control and makes faux pas/an embarrassing ass of himself.

Watch your approach: I don't even dare talk about it or it pushes his button and he shuts down.

I'll give you the shirt off my back, I just don't wanna be robbed of it. The communist spirit has taken over, they just take it.

I push that button and he goes into his mode. I watch what I say to have a good day.

SOCIAL PSYCHOLOGY IS ABOUT HYPNOSIS

Hangout culture is hookup culture, both vultures.

If you ever wanna hear some good lies, go to a funeral.

World War II and Jewish genocide wasn't about abnormal psychology but SOCIAL psychology.

It's social hypnosis that makes a whole people crazy, doing things horrendous and completely outa the ordinary.

Whatever it is I can squeeze it in unless it entails waiting. I don't wanna wait one minute for dilatory earthlings.

When you're arguing with a fool it just proves they're two. Old saying

Holocaust denial is illegal in 17 nations including Germany and Israel. Who could deny such a thing, can't they feel?

JEZEBEL SPIRIT VS. SELF-LOVE

I'd love to be her friend but not if she's gonna be a cloud without rain, a disappointment, a land without justice.

Under her tyranny all my needs were answered by arbitrariness so I adapted by strict order of the ship.

When the whole family believes in a fairytale and one doesn't, that's it--he escapes or is scapegoated.

They think they're talking to the dead so won't take any correction and will get mad at your pure doctrine.

It is essential that you love yourself and be convinced that all-else was the devil from whom you're divorced.

Self-love [for God-given talents etc] will stop shame and guilt introjected from past systems--get rid of em.

Start to love talents/qualities that are YOU to divorce from the bad image from frenemies in the human zoo.

I was so shamed I couldn't enjoy life. Drill down: If its from repented sins God doesn't even remember em.

Residual misplaced shame/guilt blocks God's work so you must blot it out and mentally replace those jerks.

DISCONFIRMATION AND LOW SELF-ESTEEM

If you never got confirmation nor made a connection [emotions rejected] it's *you* you look down on.

You never feel competent no matter what you've achieved if there wasn't that confirmation early on, basically.

That sets up a cycle of workaholism and overachievement and thus the greatest writers were the most rejected.

Art transcends fashion. Being trendy is not arty, it's just boring. Go higher, deeper, access ALL of history.

While under her tyranny I got the feeling I didn't exist--thus being dehumanized was terrifying and made me pist.

PHONY EQUALITY—OF RESULTS

Democrats only care about "equality" of results--and to get that they must remove all of our freedoms/perks.

Democrats only care about "equality" of results--and to get that they must remove all of our freedoms/get tough.

Say something mildly favorable about religion and it's "hate speech" of the worst kind in this generation.

American "intellectuals" are embarrassingly poisoned by the nonsense and dishonesty from our colleges.

These people are anti-religion/science/history/liberty and they rule our republic and schools with treachery.

They're not content to leave us alone to practice faith but take delight in compelling us to violate conscience.

This is not decay or progressivism for there is no progress--it is organized destruction. Atty. General Barr

They're trying to replace Christianity with nothing to replace it with, even secular humanism went.

I saw all youth movements as totalitarian institutions and thus I refused to join them. Lucien Lazar

THE WILL: FOR LIBERALS NOT A NICKLE

The left is obsessed with everything ugly: bathrooms, genitals, poop, blood coming out of openings.

All of em [white, black, brown] savages: spoiled rotten video game players caring for no one but themselves.

It's a spirit when people get into not caring: apathy is chic, coldblooded callousness is attractive and endearing.

Bad drivers are harrowing: There's always another car to pass, it's the ATTITUDE of passing I'm rejecting.

Bad drivers have anxious riders and good drivers have RELAXED ones and that is the very definition.

The serial passer will also get too close to other cars. He's insanely dense about what could happen of course.

ZOMBIES: SLOW AND STUPID

People have become slow and stupid--you know it and I know it, we just don't say it. Zombies, insipid.

It's a deliberate dumb-down and physically they've become squared, inelegant compared to sticks from before.

Dumbed down people are sensual, rude, shallow, in the moment pleasures but no eternal love of God.

Dumbed down people follow illogical demagoguery and slogans so incendiary that it is very scary.

Overnight people hated the Jews--the hatred spread like a wildfire. It's not abnormal but social psychology.

Why would normally decent, educated people act like that en masse? It's abnormal yes, but Social Psychology.

They're invested in the ChiComs: If America goes down they go up and that's why they hate Donald Trump.

Not everything is good--gotta get over that! In the world there is deep evil--stay away people, get the facts.

The UK is gone unless each Brit takes on three wives with four children each. Wake up quick, I beseech.

AVOID THE WORLDLY

They're involved with the world--every detail of it--while you maximize your time and are fulfilled with it.

Who's in charge? Are you letting other people dictate your schedule, wanting to keep em happy? Discharge!

Just because I CAN do it doesn't mean it's God's will that I do it--I'd rather do the thing's I'm best at.

God will be willing to give you beauty for ashes but you gotta be ready to give up the ashes. Joyce Meyer

Doing something you're not anointed to do is what you call "hard life" and forcing the fit like that brings only strife.

Every time I did something that wasn't right for me it made me absolutely miserable going against God that way.

People problems: You still don't know what they're all about--you still think they're nice when they're not.

TRUMP IS TEACHING US NOT TO HATE OURSELVES

Trump is teaching us not to hate ourselves anymore: by identifying the true enemy we love him even more.

Faith without works is dead: That's like the "Christian" who won't fight for the unborn and is culturally-led.

Bible-thump all day telling folks they're going to hell but then refuse to stand up for the unborn/under a spell.

They go along with all the vacillations/twists and turns of the liberals without a thought: dummies, all bought.

If you love God you're gonna hate the devil and everything that's going on/be unable to conform to the throng.

Antifa is composed of un-American authoritarians.

Rush Lumbaugh says things Alex Jones said two months ago and this makes Alex dangerous, ya know?

You're wildly overstepping, Mac: cuz people are afraid of losing their liberties and we're **NEVER** going back.

Time to stop being mad at the little cogs in the wheel--rise up, gird your loins, succeed: raise your eye level.

FORGET PAST OR FORGET FUTURE

Forget the past or forget your future. Forgiveness will release you for it while God punishes the vultures.

Police stand down while **ANTIFA** attacks us. We can't believe this, like Europeans we're getting anxious.

Multiculturalism means you're totally alone with no roots. It's global corporatism with whom they're in cahoots.

Their idea of "racism" is: If you love your own people its bad. No family or men, wards of the state children.

When the enemy comes against you he's really coming against God who won't put up with it/kills the plot.

WE'VE ALREADY GOT THE VICTORY

According to God I've already got the victory: what I'm doing now is walking it out--a phase called "waiting".

Resisting the devil doesn't mean you have no problems but just not acting like the devil while you've got em.

God's watching how you wait. If throwing fits it's back on the potter's wheel but if calm you'll have good fate.

If Trump isn't removed it'll **ALL** be exposed--DNC, Clinton Foundation, Barry Soetoro--so it's coming to blows.

A female genius can't trust women/has natural competition with men: she must succeed despite no friends.

Fake news media **CREATES** emotional currency then directs it as a weapon against our great president.

Stop looking up old flames and dames. Go **FORWARD** where they don't belong cuz they're insane.

You've got **ONE** life to live so don't waste it looking up old flames just cuz you can, go **FORWARD** my friend.

Thinking about them acts as **ANCHORS** to a lower level when you were a little weasel scared of the devil.

God has great and creative works for you to do cuz you're an expert in that **ONE** thing he equipped you to use.

Stop thinking of puny creeps from the past and go forward just by quitting the nasty **HABIT** of looking back.

And by **NO** means give your mind to **ARROGANT** creeps, for arrogance is the devil's biggest characteristic.

DO IT FOR THE WORK ALONE

I'm gonna put it all out there and not be concerned with the outcome. Whether they like it or not is irrelevant.

Concern with outcome has been my entire problem. It's loving the work God gave me I should be thinking of.

Like they told Andy Williams: Stop thinking about money and cars and just perfect those vocal chords.

You're not doing this great and marvelous work for the money or fame but for the pure joy of it every day.

That's how you gotta get: just into the work and perfecting it. You do that, money will come--it is promised.

Why is dressing like a slut the only thing allowed for Halloween? They want us demoralized you see.

You can't get their attention for your work. It's out there so just wait for GOD to get it from mere clerks.

ANTI-FAMILY FORCES

Global corps don't want FAMILY restricting buying or adopting the horrible, nasty goals they're advancing.

Everything they advance is anti-family, anti-nation, anti-reason, anti-creativity/flourishing in due season.

Sometimes I can hear someone yelling at me. This is an introject from the dead past which is still lingering.

Disagree with them and the young creeps get pugnacious. Hold on to true reality--get to the middle states.

Stay in L.A./Frisco you'll be swallowed up with this crap. Get to the middle states and get you some land.

I have been very hurt by God's people let alone all the heathen attacking good in the war with evil.

Never forget Jesus came to his OWN and was persecuted and crucified. He knows the pain from those who lied.

Sometimes the wounding and my RESPONSE to it shows God directing me in another way and I'm loving it.

Emotions bypass intellectual circuitry--that's why globalists evoke em but always thru staging something.

The left wants us in a civil war. They will start staging events against themselves just like always before.

They'll stage things and always blame Trump supporters. They're always into Satan and death: anti-God rockers.

They'll stab or run cars into people--that's the plan. Then things will escalate quickly with arms buildup man.

The leftist takeover is about two goals: determining outcomes and getting even with oppressors.

It's a historic low when perversion, corruption and indecency is up against normalcy. Rush Limbaugh

DEPTH AND STUDIOUSNESS

With all that assiduity my life was fulfilled in so many ways that people with tons of friends just aren't, ok?

All I did was work and study since age ten. It was deeply fascinating but when with people that was gone.

When in music whether salsa band or orchestra I felt deep soul connection but with people that was all gone.

What I learned: When a man comes to the door don't let him in cuz he'll change you and make you adapt to him.

Over-mourning a rejection is actually a leak from an earlier strata when it would mean death to the infant, yah.

Decay and the inevitability of death stalks us all. I guess this is part of all of Creations "groans".

SOCIAL PSYCHOLOGY AND THE NAZIS

Why would normally decent, educated people act like that en masse? It's Social Psychology not "abnormal", yes?

Lunacy is contagious in human beings: in monkey studies we even see mimicking when on different islands.

Scary phenomenon: Holocaust denial, minimalization and trivialization tho' in history it's the biggest thing.

France is the center of Holocaust Denial and each generation gets worse with immigration of course.

They put the holocaust on the same level with all disasters, thus denying it's uniqueness in all of human history.

By denying the holocaust they're going in favor of antisemitism--that's how serious this minimization.

25 years of Clinton/Obama domination decimated the dems--it has no vitality because it has no dissent.

Seven out of 10 Millennials say they'd vote for a socialist. Dear Lord it sounds like we've had it.

One in three sees communism as favorable. Without Civics being taught in over 40 years, schools have failed.

Fake whistleblowers were just anti-Trump insiders.

All races are different, it's ok to be white and we want America to stay the majority European alright?

SOCIAL PSYCHOLOGY AND PORN

Very few blind people join colonies of nudists. Group exposure is the hallmark of perverted cultists.

One thing about pornography is it glorifies crime and ridicules law, authority, morals and family decency.

And thus pornography leads to increased depravity and licentiousness: license to further regression.

VICE is presented as FUN. This warped idea of fun is reflected in massive births outa wedlock my son.

That the increasing crime rate reflects the increasing obscenity is surely no surprise to you or me.

Sexual materials are creating criminals faster than we have prisons to house them. It's Satan's entry point, amen?

The porn racket is challenging every parent in America as kids and their friends go behind locked doors, yah?

DEPRAVITY, GIRLY-MEN AND BETAS

Beta males or girlie men are angry, insecure, afraid of their wives or women and apprehensive of life and livin'.

Not only do we not live a second-rate life due to bad beginnings, God turns the most bad to most good, truly.

Bad memories: Just say "NO I'm not going back there, it died with Christ and I'm resurrected to a new life."

Of course now that you're in safety you gotta ruminate over the past to work it thru/to resolve all the treachery.

Only a king can not allow serial rejections to keep him down cuz he knows as a child of God he'll eventually have won.

Your dirt reflected dirt in the system. It was those muddy waters to which sin was a device to tolerate em.

SAY NO TO BAD MEMORIES

Their dirt was socially approved, yours was not so it stood out and brought on terrible reactions in your crowd.

I don't wanna think back to that old life before Jesus Christ. It's as far from me as the east is from the west.

When Satan uses my mind--his MAIN TOOL--against me, I say "NO!". NO dispels all those powers below.

Stop complaining of bad memories and learn to say NO when Satan triggers them since now you know it.

The most embarrassing things he puts in your mind, he's so talented that way knowing JUST what to say.

You were the sensitive one in those muddy waters, so you became the worst sinner vis-a-vis the others.

They were so callous and tyrannical you, in pure fright, fell into your bag and it became a groove and a drag.

Just thank GOD you're away from these people now. In safety you'll have many memories to work thru, so...

The next step is to work on self: It wasn't your fault, it was a mal-adaptation to the hostile system you're in.

The way they thought was so horrible but socially accepted and you were the scapegoat of all their stresses.

You adapted as you could and went totally blind to it. That was insanity but now you know so release it today.

It's just a blurp in time, as the generations pass all this is trivia never remembered or even ever existed.

Seeing things cosmically means eternally: in the lexicon of human suffering your biggest problem is totally petty.

OMNIPOTENT GOD ERASES SIN/THE PAST!

Our God has the capacity to ERASE the past and our sins. To make us white as snow: recognize that power now.

Just say "God, the past is tormenting me. Please ERASE it so I can do Your work and be happy".

In fact Einstein said there IS no past: time is a dimension, gone--but it's how Satan brings us down.

Those losers you hung out with were before the blood of Christ. That's your old life, unbelievable now.

You don't go back in memory/you don't go back to see em, it's erased along with all the unnecessary commotion.

Look at bad memories in an Einsteinian sense: only your sin as the reaction reinforces the memory/repeats em.

Falling into your bag of bad memories reinforces the sin you use to adapt to them--**REPENT** to erase em.

You be a new person, it is literally erased in memory and it's impossible to see the saint as a sinner, that's God's way.

There are some sins causing shame long after repentance. Bulimia is one, the recovered feels shame constantly.

Maybe she'd feel less shame had she been a fornicator, gambler or drunkard like the others--that's the game.

We're all sinners but some stand out conspicuously and he will be released by seeing this Einsteinian reality.

Who criticized me the most? A whoremonger, a loser--because I let him due to a porous border.

Who was my biggest persecutor and traitor? A drunkard, a wino, an alcoholic turned sadist, my ex-lover.

NAZI GERMANY ABNORMAL OR SOCIAL PSYCHOLOGY?

I know all about treachery and sick systems and our mal-adaptations to both and how we take on all the guilt.

People get wind of something and run with it. Suddenly people side against you and your bones feel it.

You saw how fast they turned as a group. People you knew, your brother etc. became a chicken coop.

It happened in Nazi Germany overnight as friends became foes wanting to rob, kill, replace and disgrace.

Was Nazi Germany a case of Abnormal or Social Psychology? Were they all born crazy?

As an adult it's time to take the bull by the horns. Grow up and produce cuz before you know it you'll be gone.

People will impose on you if you let em, esp. in expectations of sex. You must stand up against this.

JOYCE SEES OR TALKS TO NO ONE

At her peak Joyce Meyers won't see anyone, talk, email, phone or anything else. At age 75 she deserves this.

Joyce Meyer is my model regarding this. It's too much trouble/I just wanna produce/I don't need their lip.

They just can't keep their trap shut--their meaningless pie-hole--and inevitably offend, overreach, grab it all.

As an adult take the bull by the horns by not feeding memories from decades back--that's Satan's wreck.

There's too much to do now that our world's collapsing: make yourself ABLE by saying "NO!", zapping it.

See things cosmically, i.e. eternally: Don't get stuck in time or any era--it's dissolved in mind and not germane to ya.

You're too deep for em--don't go shallow to be noticed again, plant your seed and wait for the link to come in.

The link WILL come in. You know your work's God-driven, you felt it every moment--so too with the link hon'.

I stopped resentments about being imposed on when I heard Joyce Meyers was raped 200x by age ten.

Yes you were imposed on, but let it go. It's the human condition across world and yours was an easy road.

Unless you live in a cave you're imposed on by humans and you go insane or adapt perfectly to crowded conditions.

I was so stressed adapting to crowded conditions and WAR under the same roof I lost self/became a total lune.

I'm just interested in continuing my work in private and letting it stand on it's own, not discussing it.

It was before the blood of Christ--all forgotten now. But you must do your part: say NO when it pops up pal.

The greatest deficit in the evangelical church has been the lack of teaching about the devil. Martin Jones

Teaching about the devil is ultra-important since people perish from lack of knowledge: FALLEN.

Jack or Joe ain't your enemy at all. One of the main ways Satan attacks us is through people who love us.

HINT: People hurt us by wanting to take care of themselves and wanting you to do what they want you to do.

SATAN USES THOSE CLOSEST

We care about em/want their approval so when Satan uses those closest to obstruct us it's even more lethal.

Obstruction is it: Get thee behind me Satan. You are an offense, a hindrance, and you're in my way. Matt 16

You [FRIEND/FAMILY] are being used by the devil to prevent me from performing God's will.

Living way out in a ghost town I was a sitting duck whenever they came around but now I'm protected/owned.

You've got to make yourself strong--that is, RESILIENT--because trouble will come/ya gotta be ready son.

THEY ALWAYS WANT SOMETHING

You can't trust a lying/thieving Jezebel or one who brings division from good but with evil she justifies it all.

When she/he came around it was nothing but trouble immediately. A drag, rut, jam and offense to me.

They always wanted something, there was something sneaky about em. Sickening, I didn't trust them.

As handsome as Lucifer he could be a coldblooded killer and you can't let em in without a social checker.

The loser: If you let em in he'll rise up against you or try to get money outa you. Beta, gigolo, user, P-U.

After she came around I always felt insulted/violated, like a spirit, and later there was always things missing.

The loser seeks to INVADE you--often with friends--to make you do his will. He has no personal power just social.

BAD MEMORIES: JUST SAY NO

I just twitched and shuddered remembering a noxious event 30 years ago then remembered to say "NO!"

God doesn't want you to suffer with all these memories, you've gotta know that to let em go/reject the low.

Why am I always relieved when viewing a fifties movie or doc? It's another time, a relief from constant smut.

If I am nothing I have no shame so I stay at nothing and that makes me "apt" to receive creative and a blessing.

You've gotta know the devil's outa ya so stop with the shame or that wimpy pout on ya.

You gotta go >16 hours a day in a complete fast. Water only, it's easy and it's like having a blast.

Multicultural diversity means these things: tension, mistrust and conflict, not "strength".

The truth is: People don't like diversity. The human animal wants to be around people like themselves. Jared Taylor

America's "greatest strength" is more like a flood, fire or hurricane--you must insure against it/always payin'

All "diversity training" in big corporations doesn't extinguish prejudice--it just promotes it. Jared Taylor

DIVERSITY KILLS TRUST

Diversity kills community trust. They do less volunteer work, less confidence in local gov and fewer friends.

Diversity training doesn't work--it promotes it. Harvard Business Review Study

Diversity is like a flood--you must insure against discrimination suits happening here and abroad.

Chinese universities don't have bloat, waste and stupidity built into the system--they aren't cursed with diversity.

The "hate map" is an absolute scam. It finds as much hate as possible to make as much money as they can.

Stop taking orders from people who hate you. Stay "yes" to your friends/"no" to your enemies many or few.

Progressives demand we bow down to political correctness the rules of which only they determine.

In this day and age you gotta handle success like a crate of eggs. You can lose all your great gains in a minute, ok?

When I think of you I think "that was an earlier era" when I experienced what's going on in America, hell ya.

You were my Ph.D in the Streets--before you I never knew such evil existed or the will to destroy your own sista.

YOU WERE MY PH.D. IN THE STREETS

She disagreed with his politics so ruined him. She didn't like my viewpoints so wrecked my reputation.

It wasn't as bad as war or prison but you were a helluva lesson of treachery/deception: my Ph.D. in the Streets.

They giggle like adolescents over the length of their member or their latest hookup, that's this era.

They actually think people are always the same but every generation is different and I won't take this, ok?

They like to be here cuz my life is ordered and simple. They don't have that anywhere else I marveled.

We live in a fallen world--MOST people are immoral. That may not mean much to you but it's phenomenal.

Heaven-hell is no big thing to you now, but wait til you die and get a big surprise--don't take that chance guys.

There's right and wrong, you need to know where to draw the line. In a fallen world MOST are immoral swine.

How dare you say I wasted time. Those were my dry, silent years with it all happening underground full-time.

OPEN SEASON ON WHITE PEOPLE NOW

Let's go out and attack whites who are inherently bad--that's the anti-white atmosphere the left created.

My family tried to wipe out my memory let alone my life. Honor Killing Victim

She was to be erased from the face of the earth. There was to be no trace of her.

He beheaded thousands, raped and murdered little girls, and Wash. Post calls him an "austere religious scholar."

The reality: it's open-season on white people as crime stats show--and it's very dangerous I hope you know.

I don't like being approached. I like being alone, I'm a loner avoiding the throng--I think best as just one.

Since my best ideas occur when I'm left alone or happily at home, I just MUST avoid absolutely everyone.

ENERGY WASTE OF SENSITIVES

God is done with you playing second fiddle or being hidden under a bushel--when it's time He'll let ya know.

He'll let you know when you're ready to show and patience is very wise on this to save from embarrassment.

Sensitives hate loud noises, socials/crowds, hangers/small talk, chaos/disorder, TV, artificial lights, smells, violence.

I let a small offense [which the perpetrator didn't even remember] turn into a ROOT of bitterness.

Lady on sex: "In the times I let it casually happen when young I never got over it, feeling inauthentic and wrong."

We only have so much energy each day--why waste it offended, holding grudges, feeling resentment?

I need that valuable energy for my dreams, my destiny, my household. Not gonna waste it anymore on you all.

Mature attitude: Someone did me a great wrong but I'm not at all worried, I know God will pay him back.

I have no more chip on my shoulder, I know God is fighting my battles and He will be my vindicator.

BITTERNESS/ANGER ARE CONTAMINATES/DRAINS

Bitterness and anger are contaminates not just drains. Now you'll get your joy back and take the reins.

We are created in the image of God: He made us to be happy, healthy, whole and secure--not bitter.

God didn't make us to be bitter, angry, resentful--we need to get rid of what is contaminating our stream.

Resentment that someone stole $100 keeps you from making a million because life is a pie--amen?

Forgive them. They hurt you once, don't allow them to continue to--let it go, cast your care, enjoy the view.

The future is vindication, healing, new beginnings--that's where God is. So don't go back He's not in the past.

God is waiting in the future--"there"--so if we're still hung up "here" anchored by resentments there is failure.

God allowed my buttons to be pushed until I learned. It was my fault not His that it took so many years.

No theoretician can fit any discussion group without causing em to rise up against him--the victim.

GENIUS CANNOT FIT

He sees the whole, they don't. By drawing threads together it causes them to bolt/reject odd man out.

As soon as they rear up there's disrespect and I exit the group. I will not stay around these chicken coops.

Your problem was expecting more from family than they could give. Like asking a legless man to run a race.

Hypersensitives are more hurt by criticism so avoid it by people pleasing, criticizing self first or avoiding the source.

Can we absorb emotions/spirits from an online discussion group? Absolutely, positively--escape chicken coop.

It's not that they're not important but that you can't take anyone with you--we come in alone/go out alone.

Self-pity is a wasted day that just keeps you stuck in the same spot. I've been guilty of that: thinking back.

The world will flow in so you have to be the one to put the breaks on/establish boundaries of a hypersensitive.

They ask me why I'm so judgmental--it ain't for me to judge but I'm gonna say what I see. Kanye West

I'm tired of being alone yet people drive me crazy. I'm between lives--a test between treachery and victory.

She treated me not as a home but a storage facility for her stuff and her friends--before boundaries this happened.

This shouldn't be an issue but since they broke thru I have PTSD from the impositions and so I lecture to you.

I don't know why I attracted the m-asses but it was a great lesson about being famous and how to manage it.

PROTECT YOURSELF AS IF FAMOUS

I didn't know enough to protect myself as a famous person, I was still Mrs. Hostess and didn't feel a reason.

I probably even wanted their company at times, as cabin fever is a real thing and can rapidly drive you nuts.

I felt them coming at me, wanting in my house, wanting something, always wanting something...lush/louse.

A famous person with a mansion and OF COURSE a wall and locked gate would never face this fate.

But I wasn't thinking like that--I wanted that in the future but ignored the blight of invaders where I sat.

I was renting this old cabin, I couldn't put a fence up. So I had to endure the torture for decades of mean crud.

I did not know what people were like. I'd lived in an ivory tower or sheltered with Christians and decent folk.

It was so horrible--how they acted, the presumptuousness, the arrogant impositions, taking things, hating me.

They're in their fifties now, wonder what they're like. Did schools just temporarily create delinquents? Yikes

Now demons are entering five year olds thru drag queen story times and learning how to twerk by fiends.

GOD IS JUSTICE, SO RELAX!

In order to forgive you MUST know God is justice and he'll get em. Leave it to Him and forgive to live again.

When did I ask for your opinion? Not only that, you're just someone who happened to come with my friend.

God will deliver justice when you forgive em or stop taking revenge yourself. Forgive, readjust, God does it.

Act famous: don't see anyone unless they have a helluva lot to give you. Porous borders is masochism too.

Everyone says they're so woke but they follow the rules about what woke's supposed to be. Kanye West

You'll become famous with the right comportment, which is to not see anyone unless they're the top, the cream.

Losers flow in to use you wherever you are in the game. It's just as easy to marry a rich man as a poor one ma'am.

Part of my path was 16 years total isolation in the wilderness then ten more adapting to marriage.

ALONE, NEVER LONELY OR BORED

I'm never lonely nor bored. The more isolated I get the more that is the truth, nothing and no one's as cool.

I learned to live on a 1000 acres alone for 7 months in the dark. To conquer these fears was really a lark.

But the worst part was when people came to my house. It was so aggravating it was solved only by a fence.

Don't blame them for your lack of boundaries. It's a jungle madhouse out there--you failed to self-protect, see?

I considered myself a free thinker but I was thinking exactly what I was supposed to. woke Millennial

How I became a racist, sexist and misogynist: I voted Republican not as part of a victim group I guess.

A king has no friends, only followers. The Irishman

70% want socialism and they're very vindictive when it comes to punishments, like their friends the ChiComs.

Have patience, everything's in a sequence. Just sort drawers/watch movies while you wait for success.

When I left a sheltered home for college I panicked, entering muddy waters where sex was expected.

One in three sees communism as favorable. Without Civics being taught in over 40 years, schools have failed.

PATIENCE: IT ALL HAPPENS IN A SEQUENCE

Everything happens in a sequence and you can't predict this. Just move into place as God instructs.

It's a matter of your SEASON: At a certain point God turns on the spout and it all flows in. Before then, nothing.

It's not that you've lost their attention but that they've been drawn away and it's good riddance I'd say.

If a pervert in a park exposes genitals it was 10 years in prison but it's ok for drag queen story-time villains.

Drag queen story time is a pedophile invasion in organized increments sexualizing children more each minute.

Praising ISIS leader while bashing Trump: It's just bizarre and surely shows who they are.

The best talents ripen late but that's also when the ageist comments ramp up so <u>draw lines</u> or bad fate.

They take your life over having to respond to disinformation. It would be constant, refuse em.

HIX POLITIX

Relax gun laws to help us good guys get geared up against drug cartels who ALL have machine guns.

Drug cartels and other criminals have machine guns and grenade launchers-- what is our defense sirs?

Mexico: Total prohibition against guns yet highest crime rate in the world. That's where this is going for sure.

Warren and Bernie want us to pay for criminals getting genitals cut off--that's the democrat religion now.

Sure sex is normal but it's not for children, exposed to it before they're even thinking about it.

It's worse than being an alcoholic: being a WIFE of one. For every alki there are four people sick/it's no fun.

He's just being himself but the problem is he has a camera on him. See the value of divine patience, amen.

He had to smash me down to the proper comportment vis-a-vis him. There was a click in my head from then.

ALONE AT HOME I SOAR

At home I'm in my own element and space. When in a crowd I'm assaulted like sirens loud/read thoughts.

A cat in a roomful of rocking chairs--that's how I always felt when imposed on by losers but alone, I soar.

What I've achieved so far: a great marriage/house, a fence/locked gate and wisdom to avoid bad fate.

You can't ever impose on me again/you can't ever bring your [army] friends-- I'm protected by a high fence.

You can't ever come over and make me adapt to you and your sidekicks too. I have solitude, a wall and my view.

Jezebel always gets her men against you. She always calls you the shrew/she's always got a bug to work thru.

My true destiny began the day I got a locked gate and wall. For the first time in my life I felt authentic and whole.

Trump has a bond with his supporters that no one can break, it's beyond understanding and it's innate.

NOTHING WORSE THAN A MULTICULTURALIST

There is nothing worse than a multiculturalist cuz he'll try any cruel bizarre thing to be trendy but we are patriots.

The fat gay muckbanger "Nikocado" eats dogs boiled alive. He's so cool, trendy and multicultural--no jive.

Globalist-corporatist news media are just left wing activists disguised as journalists and they are collapsed!

There were times in history where things became so bad morally there was only one need: a moral manual.

It may be better to see him as your imaginary friend, not your guardian angel or spirit guide--it is heretical.

The churches have fallen cuz women have rule em and it's pagan. Like always, they think it's good they're doin.

Music: Who Feels It Knows It. Etana

You robbed me then expect me to forget it: fact. Are you kidding? I would never think of taking you back.

The pagan female church leaders forgive everything and draw no lines--to their heretical minds that's "kind".

Forgiving without repentance is how you create criminals. It's happening across the land mostly with moms.

Of course how could they draw lines when they're so immoral themselves? Embarrassing, debauched.

How could they instill morality, when they're sluts who trust in trash? It's three generations of this I guess.

He's an aspiring billionaire but currently a stay-at-home step dad, and this is happening across the land.

It helped me to know there wasn't one I was mad at, it was being imposed on period cuz I was a deep empath.

DEEP EMPATHS AND RIDICULE

You gotta realize the battle is in the mind and work on those memories. When they come up, deny.

You're not hurting them by being so unforgiving, their lives go on. It's a battle in the mind, keeping you down.

The prevalent ageism is all based on SMV [sexual market value] so it's irrelevant to you--separate your view.

A Deep Empath feels slaughtered by criticism or ridicule so they adapt by various means: isolation/insulation.

Could be Meghan Markle is a deep empath not arrogant as I thought. In that case she **REALLY** hurts a lot.

A deep empath is tortured by gossip and ridicule and it's the reason genius dies early from drugs/alcohol.

There was no way I could conform or would choose to but the odd-girl-out is tortured as too out of the norm.

The unique can't endure remarks from retards so become increasingly isolated seeming even more bizarre.

It helped immensely to know it wasn't Tom, Dick or Harry I was mad at but being imposed on by **ALL** idiots.

A person is famous without being famous--the "well-known unknown." If he can handle that God opens more.

PROFESSIONAL SHOW-OFFS/PUTDOWN ARTISTS

It's a guy who's **NOT** in control or a naive know-it-all who brandishes his role and I'm really sick of y'all.

Dentists making personal comments: When you're in the chair he has control--just say NO and find a real pro.

Professional men feel compelled to ridicule when they're in control: Even if younger they get way too bold.

When you're in the dental chair he says anything he wants to you. Get a new professional and a new view.

If every time you go to the dentist it takes three months to heal from his words, find a new professional girls.

Pros are here to do a job--that's what they're hired for. Anything else [silly remarks] is grounds to fire, no?

Housekeeper kept saying "you look so good for your age" and was fired for her backhanded insults all day.

Classic black Bermuda shorts to the knees are perfectly fine but not in Mormon country--Oh, how shameful!

I finally said: I will NOT have this imposed on me again. Find a new professional man, don't ever give in.

JEZEBEL TAKES OFFENSE BEING DENSE

Cuz she's dumbed, Jezebel so EASILY takes offense then gets all her men against you--no longer an enigma.

Professional man with the upper hand: I'm not gonna put up with your crap like your wife has to man.

Professional man would compete by attacking my vulnerabilities but I'm smarter than hillbillies.

Dentists just can't resist once they get you in the chair. They'll pour their theories/remarks in for sure.

Making rude, impertinent, condescending/insubordinating remarks just cuz they have you in the chair.

They'll use everything against you, use their position to ridicule you then take your money too.

I've forgiven you cuz God said to but that doesn't mean I have to be around you, ever ever again--WHEW

Forgiveness is a selfish thing, it releases us to success. I can't have that if I'm a resentful, seething mess.

SO SICK OF THE LOW CLASS MASS ASS

They called me ungrateful, another enigma. Until I realized it was cuz they didn't want me to have anything at all.

It just takes one famous person to endorse you--just that ONE--then suddenly your sales take off, hon'.

An immature or angry "professional" will be compelled to abuse you once you're under his control.

Jezebel: It's a dangerous game she plays. You don't give her what she wants and her men will make you pay.

You get so sick of the low class mass ass you go strictly solitude then ATTRACT the right--that's the highest.

All that early fame was a season I needed to keep the stoke going. But now I'm doing it for myself. Tanner Hall

The ageism is just terrible. Just cuz you're reached a certain age they make cruel remarks every day.

Ageism is much worse than racism but since it's all about the youth they never think of that man.

JEZEBEL IS VILE AND VICIOUS

Jezebel is a vile and vicious slut who uses "her men" against you cuz inside she doesn't measure up.

Jezebel will always have a problem with you cuz you want order but she wants to steal you blind too.

Once Jezebel sends her man against you anything can happen for the Jezebel Spirit is entirely cruel.

Jezebel Spirit will kill your dogs to get back at you. She wants nothing you love to distract from her feud.

Evil never reviews what it's doing and feels invincible until the moment it runs out of gas. Alex Jones

SUDDENLY they see they are standing on NOTHING.

Systems theory: all mental illness is rooted in attachment trauma--we are framed by the system, esp. momma.

I didn't call you a beast I said you should preach. A lot of meaning is lost in email, ya think?

It's hard to win arguments with a smart person but it's impossible to win one with a stupid person. Bill Murray

People are stupid cuz they go along with each other: That's a system but only the smart can see the bad weather.

Success will just appear one day. Like a thief in the night, suddenly it's a new world and everything's changed—all right!

Every time you wanna go higher your flesh has gotta come down way lower. God's words to Joyce Meyer

I'm always happy when I'm working, doing my own thing. It's like another world: cornucopia of the right brain.

It's impossible to win arguments with a stupid person and females are dumbed thru conformity [that's the reason].

GUILTY CONSCIENCE IS LOST BOLDNESS

"Sowing to the flesh brings ruin, decay and destruction." Every Friday night produced Saturday's NO-FUN.

In our seared consciences we did stuff that didn't bother us but as we grow in God we look back SO embarrassed.

And the day will come in the End Times when people will think good is evil and evil is good, understood?

I'm so glad I know its wrong, rather than zombies accepting how they're programmed by the Hollywood throng.

I set before you life and death. Choose life so that you and your descendants may live. Deut. 30: 19

The biggest mistake we make is thinking we can play with fire and not get burned. Suddenly you're dead girl.

Guilty conscience is a major problem cuz it blocks necessary boldness--they can't get it thru osmosis.

If we feel guilty/condemned with guilty conscience, we're not gonna go boldly to the throne, not a chance.

If our conscience is sweet/does not condemn us then before God we have confidence and assurance.

THE WAITING PHASE IS A TEST

Have it all available and if they wish to drill down they will-- when they see your depth they'll be thrilled.

This is where FAITH WHILE YOU WAIT comes in. You put it all out there and stay hopeful tho' there's nothin'.

Of course any artist wants two things which are justified: remuneration and recognition, I never lied.

We must now divide on moral lines cuz one bad apple ruins the whole crate but if we do that it's called "hate".

Fallen Hero Syndrome: Need courage to get back up again. This is the path of most writers and discoverers needing humblin'.

We all have bad things happen and if Satan keeps loading that old worn-out movie our whole lives can be ruined.

"I'm sure he's forgiven him cuz he's a Christian and to prevent another deadly aneurism but God'll get 'im."

Wait for the RIGHT link to come to your site then drill down to the multifaceted windows of your brilliant insights.

You've proven yourself and completed your work. Now take a needed VACA-- an R and R after all those jerks.

Because we got educated via people problems, forgiveness is our ONE burden and greatest lesson.

Why I've always thought I'd make it: I love God, He is in me and this is what I do naturally so He'll bless it, see?

Choose a path, set a goal. Achieve it then shatter it. Tanner Hall

EVERYONE'S BAD, NO ONE GOOD

Please be tolerant as your culture dies.

I took his crap until that moment I didn't. With the upper hand he couldn't resist to shit-shot/call me a bigot.

As I look back men were bad but women were horrible yet few can see this-- told it's men who are awful.

Actually, everyone's bad and no one's good. Jesus even said He wasn't--only God--and we're all hoods.

Loser: "I really wanna go to bed early, get up early, stop partying and buckle down but life gets to me".

We are going thru a great derangement. People are irrational, feverish and herd-like. Douglas Murray

There's an extraordinary lack of courage at the moment--the courage to say what is true. Douglas Murray

WHITE PEOPLE REPLACEMENT

in 1960 whites were 90% of America and in 2040 they'll be a minority--a catastrophic change to our reality.

White people just wanna be left alone. That is not "white supremacy" but we're called it constantly ya know.

It is clearly a change of one population replacing another. Whites are told NOT to resist this suicide either.

Most non-whites build non-desirable societies and that's why they're trying to escape those failures today.

Failed societies busting into Europe and desiring to live with them is the natural push of demography, friends.

Unless whites are willing to say "I'm sorry, our ancestors built this for US" they'll be overwhelmed/over-run.

The replacement population won't have our interests at heart--like the <u>treatment of animals</u> for a start.

The majority of immigrants are staled in failed societies and want to come and join successful western ones.

The reality is whites are being replaced. But if we describe this reality it is called "racist".

It is without precedent in human history that the dominant group says "ok, just come and take over our country."

INVASION WITHOUT ANY DEFENSE

Usually invasion/conquering takes overwhelming force, but now it's just "come and take everything that is ours."

The idea that race is just a social construct is so obviously wrong only a dumbed pop can be convinced it's true.

White people hang their head over slavery yet it was all over the world and over there they ended it too.

It's ultra-important to maintain cultural coherence and homogeneity--so now we can expect catastrophe.

The fat gay muckbanger "Nikocado" eats dogs boiled alive. He's so cool, trendy and multicultural--no jive.

Your will: not a nickel to the family liberals or it's supporting evil.

Children of the lie: the liberal media, the democrats, the RINOs, never-Trumpers and black race hustlers.

The combo of extremism and stupidity is fostering anti-white racism as Millennials join in this treachery.

YES WE CAN JUDGE, AND SHOULD

Oh yes we CAN judge other practices, that's the meaning of being a PATRIOT: pride in knowing your way is best.

If there's no huge benefit to telling the truth but an enormous COST it's darn hard being a patriot.

We need to open a path so sensible people can speak boldly about truths we knew until yesterday. Douglas Murray

Genetic mental illness comes thru with stress or sin. Otherwise we may be normal like God's children.

Warren can't say "medicare for all" for the primary then cut back for the general--another deceiver that's all.

Where ignorance is bliss it is folly to be wise. Thomas Gray

No one is more hated than those who speak the truth. Plato

If you are a child of Satan who is a liar--you believe lies. That defines the domain of darkness we must deny.

THE TRUTH HURTS SO IS BESMERCHED

A milquetoast sentimental approach to Jesus will offend no one in the kingdom of darkness so it's approved of.

It's a mystical reality where people have gone so far into lies and deception they deny the [gender] obvious.

Reason is just a chain of cause-and-effect realities. Not 0 + 0 = everything, which is the current insanity.

The more a society drifts from truth the more it will hate those who speak it. George Orwell

All efforts to legalize sin are collective groups trapped in lies and deception trying to make their sin normal.

You can get a Ph.D. in this kind of folly but you're still a fool. John MacArthur

When God "gives you over" brother you enter a hell on earth--you've lost your cover and none will answer.

Free will and predestination reconciled: You can choose to fulfill God's Great Plan or miss it thru sin.

When men go their own way: This is the cycle in human history, creating their own Gods who say it's all-ok.

They love their sins so suppress the truth and make sure you do too or they'd have to face they're fools.

Given over: There's a time when God says "I'm done with you"--as a society or personally you're screwed.

GOD GIVES EM UP TO DEGRADING PASSIONS

Since they exchanged the truth of God for a lie God gave em over to the lusts of their flesh and impurity.

When God gives em up to degrading passions there's an explosion of immorality and a sexual revolution, see?

They worship the creature--like man--rather than the Creator who is blessed forever and ever, amen?

How do we know when God gives over an entire nation? There's always a moral/sexual revolution explosion.

With this explosion of immorality from the sixties bodies were dishonored--now we see the results, ugly.

Our entire culture is given over to immorality. The music, the sitcoms, the women's shows of pure lunacy.

WOMEN CAVE IN LAST

Historically women are the last to cave in to immorality due to mothering instinct and need men's protection.

You think I'd have this wonderful protection and home if I believed in lesbianism? No way, he's a good man.

Women are stupid to cave into this but losing male protection isn't important--they have the women.

Before you learn the lesson of fame [insulation] you're still out there in the game and will inevitably pay.

I didn't like his tone--that's all it took. I'm been here before and know the signs of disrespect from kooks.

Divine judgment sequence in a nation given over: a sexual revolution, a homosexual revolution, then The End.

God gave em over to a "depraved" mind: a mind that doesn't function like a man thinking he's a woman.

A DEPRAVED MIND GETS KOOKY IDEAS

Now they're even accommodating this insanity with bizarre medical procedures, drugs and surgeries.

Liberals: not only do the same but give hearty approval to those who practice them--like Bill Clinton.

This society will approve of your perversion but it will not allow you to tell the truth. John MacArthur

As believers we have the formidable task of bringing down fortresses. We're to be killers of giants like feminists.

A "fortress" is any anti-God speculation. You've heard it, everyone thinks they know what's goin' on.

KILLED BY OUR LIE FORTRESS

A fortress becomes their prison which becomes their tomb. They're "fortified" to criticism/armed to respond.

Evil ideologies are any elevated thing raised up against the knowledge of God and they're always flawed.

As believers we're making war on LIES by which people are imprisoned. It makes em angry but we're persistent.

Yes they will feel great offense as you grab them out of a burning house. Anger even, so expect it all.

There's an intimate connection between sin and the LIES used to justify that beloved sin.

There are eternally damning consequences to those who DIE in the fortress of their own lies, so please...

"There's a lot more I could say" is what pastor always says when he's run out of material. lol

She said "why don't you just write a book that everyone likes?" So I did and no one liked it.

I wrote a book on the love of God which is SELECTIVE--that's why no one liked it.

Due to impact of false teachers there may be few believers left if we don't fight for The Faith: the Truth.

The false teachers in the church deny the Lord's rule in our life and also the Lordship of the Son Jesus Christ.

They create the kind of Christianity that does not denounce people's sins. They just wanna get along/be all-lovin'.

The false teachers invading the church attack obedience, purity and holiness and are ok with sin/dirtiness.

Anyone propagating error has no doctrine of holiness--just a false dogma of non-sanctification [ok with scum/a mess].

Without holiness no man sees the Lord. Hebrew 12: 14.

Schools/media are ideological protective zones where their sins are safe: hell is real and they're the gate.

You die young or you get older--there's nothing in between so enjoy benefits of each stage, like getting bolder.

WOMEN: IT'S NOT REALLY HER

Women have gone crazy calling attention to themselves rather than modestly humbling under a husband.

When women take over a culture men become weak and when men are made weak they can be conquered.

When women ascend to power men become increasingly weaker and the vulnerability escalates from there.

Women are not to preach/should shut up in the church but are loudmouth tyrants when the opposite occurs.

As men become weak they fall by the sword, living out the curse of Genesis 3: thanks women your city's in ruin.

When conservative husband is cast outa the family, wifey instills liberalism into the kids: sickly cyclicity.

The root of mental illness is currently the mother since she's there, she's a liberal feminist and nuttier.

DAD IS DEMONIZED

Dad is gone--he's been pegged/demonized cuz he sees it's globalism and women's shows as pure mayhem.

People aren't inferior cuz they've gotten older but your ageist comments are very telling you trendy faker.

Empowering women makes weak men and weak men makes everyone vulnerable to danger, amen?

They talk about how strong they are but prickliness and "acting strong" becomes bitchiness all day long.

It's childish, young, inexperienced women who are ascending into power. Lord come this hour!

Oh My people: their oppressors are children and women rule over them. We're in so much trouble man.

When you overthrow the divine order the results are always disastrous, so women: find a man you can respect.

Not judging women/children but it's a divine judgement on a nation when its women and children are in power.

In the New Testament there was no woman apostle, pastor, prophet, elder, chapter author or sermon giver.

It was all men--that's the divine order. Get used to it, it's God's will--just talk to your husband about it girl.

A FALLEN NATURE SEEKS TO CONTROL

Built into the curse on us all is women's innate fallen desire to overpower her husband and take control.

BUT a gentle and quiet spirit is precious in the sight of God.

Since a women's fallen nature seeks to control, they can make life pretty miserable for y'all.

Women: No preaching, no teaching and no leading position in the church for it was Adam first created, then Eve.

It was not Adam who was deceived but the woman who then fell into transgression--that's evil man.

As a woman, what can I then do? Create a home and write the lyrics of hymns or nursery rhymes, which this is.

A woman out from protection of her head is vulnerable. I was thrown to wolves once, that's all I wanna know.

Due to our tendencies to kindness, mercy/care we become more vulnerable when unprotected or in fear.

Just think of the multitudes of modern women without a father or husband to protect them from deception.

They have only their girlfriends--blind leading the blind--or women's shows that are wrong, nutty, unkind.

Eve sinned because she was deceived by Satan but Adam sinned cuz he couldn't live without her, amen.

Role reversals: with women deceived bad things happen: men are made weak then worst things happen.

The whole human race went down when Adam listened to Eve. Tamper with God's order and you will grieve.

WHEN WOMEN RULE THERE IS CHAOS

When women take over the chaos is unending. They get advice from each other and it's anti-male friend.

By Adam giving his heart to Eve he becomes weaker then plunges the whole human race into corruption.

Fallen men and women are equally sinful. Adam loved Eve so much he sinned willfully--men need us girl.

Again, it's her fallenness--her fallen nature--that drives her to overpower her husband and show ugly anger.

Feminists boast men come from women. Not true--man comes from God and women by God out of man.

Ordered godly society: Men lead, feed, protect and provide; women support and nurture; children obey.

Sensitive female prayed: Lord I can't forget being imposed on, remove memories of flawed--anger blocks me God.

But now the world's made up of individuals, not families. Marriage means little and what a cultural tragedy.

Individualism has so perverted culture and the church that leaders are increasingly rejecting God's true word.

REBELLIOUS FEMALE PREACHERS

Rebellious female pastors FLOOD the church in male roles just as it's happening in the secular world.

Rebellious female pastors storm the stage yelling their sermons--pacing back and forth, it's embarrasin'

At the bottom of the social game is who's superior to who. Status tension drives some to drink but instead I *grew.*

But now you'll be a great success, since:

Chance favors a prepared mind. You study all your life then suddenly a group needs skills only you can provide.

Chance favors a prepared mind: just keep saying that man. Do your part then by pure coincidence it's <u>The End.</u>

Sin = demons. Repentance = whole again. Sin = demons. Repentance = whole again. Keep saying that friend.

MUST SEE THRU TV HERESIES: WORD AND FAITH

Once the older Jezebel got me in her car she rose up against me and acted like a Nazi prison guard.

Liberalism in 2020: expanded health care, strong response to climate change and protecting minority rights.

Word and faith heresy is based on "new thought": whatever you think/say attracts the same to you.

Repackaging old heresies: the "inspired" word and faith movement are plagiarists of each other really.

I can't create anything with my mind. I can only ask God and He will say "yes, no or not now" cuz He's kind.

Despite what Benny Hinn/Creflo Dollar says, only God can "speak things into existence".

The word and faith preachers elevate themselves to the Christ level, saying they can control the weather.

The word and faith movement is just as much a theological cult as Mormons or Jehovah Witnesses.

Cultic doctrine cloaked in Christianese: that's all it is. But it's god is weak not great, a cloud without rain.

At the heart of the word of faith/prosperity gospel is the "little gods" doctrine--the jealous desire of Satan.

Satan wanted to be just like God--does this not sound like the cultic TV preachers revving the audience up?

The "little gods" theory on TV is actually a doctrine of demons and the egotistical basis of all heresies.

Their reasoning: if we're Gods we can't be poor nor sick. That's the connection right there but it's a trick.

It's a different gospel but its why they hold onto it so tenaciously: we should all be rich gods naturally.

The allure of health and wealth is what makes this movement so appealing and dangerous as well.

The prosperity gospel says "come to Jesus--He'll make you healthy and wealthy", the desires of everybody.

The **TRUE** gospel: you're in sin and the wrath of God resides in you until you repent and it's all removed.

We're not promised perfect health or money but persecution and that's not as popular honey.

Escaping the wrath of God is why we come to Jesus, not the false conversions coming from wanting riches.

SOFTENING OF SIN HERESY

Related to their emphasis on health and wealth is their "softening of sin"--they don't talk about it friends.

They mention sin in a casual superficial way but never go deeply into it-- mankind's entire problem, skipped.

Their idea of repentance is to go "from thinking negatively to thinking positively"--folks, that's not repentance.

By their definition of repentance we could simply repent by joining the Optimist's Club, it's so ridiculous.

It's impossible to think positively if in sin, cuz sin contains it's own punishment--the mental trash bin.

Its not about a sunnier outlook on life for true repentance is granted TO us-- then we have a change of mind.

When God grants repentance good deeds and fruit are a natural outcome of that/can't be faked: fact.

They deny God's sovereignty: like Jesse Duplantis said he was "asked by God" for his opinion--who's he kiddin?

God doesn't need our permission for a thing, He does what He wants when He wants cuz He's the Almighty.

He who wins souls is wise but he who thinks he can counsel God is a fool from false preacher's lies.

Instead of wasting energy complaining of humans, know human nature and protect yourself from ruin.

Read the Psalms and Proverbs to know human nature. That's the Manual for Superior Men to mature.

Protect yourself from a buncha creepy users rather than the false church calling em "good", the religion lovers.

THEY DARKEN GOD'S. COUNSEL WITH ADD-ONS

Who is this who darkens My counsel with words without knowledge--who does this man think he is?

They're not saved because you can't be indwelt with the Holy Spirit and teach these kinds of blasphemies.

If a saved Christian spouted these heresies the Holy Spirit would be screaming inside it's all so spiritual snide.

God must be glorified, holy and sanctified cuz mankind is so sinful i.e. rotten, filthy, gabby and unkind.

But the false church glorifies man [little god] and diminishes God: clouds without rain, boring.

The women rose up in the church and now it's people-worshipping, kissing/hugging while gossiping.

When the men ruled the church correctly there was no hugging or chattering in the sanctuary honey.

When the loser thought he had a reason to hate he became implacable, merciless, dismissive/we were 86ed.

GOD GIVES THE ONLY CHANGE IN YOU

When God saves someone He changes them and leads them into truth--error lasts only for a season too.

The fans of word/faith prosperity preaching don't have this inner illumination of truth or will leave when they do.

When God saves em He moves em out of these heretical movements and it doesn't take long after awakening.

They learn the difference between inputed {God granted) and infused righteousness: WORKS like Catholics.

Here I'm saved yet the Mormons and Catholics tell me I gotta do all these things to get it--it's not legit.

Instead of bad memories of what was done to me, I thank God for the lesson I obviously needed to be free.

God is the author of all things and allows things to happen so His glory shines forth more in comparison.

They diminish the status of Christ so they may elevate themselves to His same status: watch this.

We are gods: In de-elevating Christ they're on His level and can perform constant money-making miracles.

When they read in the bible where it says "I AM" they just smile and say "I AM TOO"--what a false lure.

False preachers say Jesus was just the first fruit and as children of God we're all EQUAL--to Jesus too.

We are children of God through **ADOPTION** and there's only one begotten: Jesus Christ, God's true Son.

They say Jesus was "just a man" until God put His spirit inside of Him--implying we can too, as **EQUAL**.

They have a different God, gospel and Jesus. It's not enough to believe in Jesus but the **RIGHT** Jesus.

Mormons, Jehovah's Witnesses and even Muslims believe in Jesus--you gotta believe in the **RIGHT** Jesus.

STOP COMPLAINING ABOUT PEST CONTROL LESSONS

Stop complaining about pests, your teachers. You needed the lesson or you'd never have been there.

Just cuz it happened obviously you needed the lesson so thank God for your teachers those pagans.

Masculine republics give way to feminine democracies and femme democracies give way to tyranny.

As soon as you asserted yourself they were gone. That's all it took, you were a milquetoast lily before then.

Stop going over events in your mind. Those aren't the point for as soon as you stood up they declined.

As soon as you learned the lesson you took the reins and persecutors lessened so forget the bad events son.

He kept coming to the door as I remained nice/indecisive but when I said **NO** he went away/came no more.

All civilizations begin with growth and momentum then end with decline and extinction mimicking nature I reckon.

SEE THE PAST AS A LESSON ONLY

Learn the essential lessons and then let the past--your Ph.D in the streets-- go as if it never happened.

Don't keep mulling it over with anger cuz then your knowledge gains turn to losses: failure/ill fame.

Thank you _______ for what I learned from your harassment was enough to fill 103 books about neurotic asses.

The feeling of being imposed on will never go away cuza you so I keep writing to deal with it--thank you!

Thank your past no matter how aggravating cuz it made you strong and unswerving with highest boundaries.

No you can't hook up your RV on my land cuz the last time you invited all your friends without asking man.

FROM TOTAL VICTIM TO BOOK DATA

What I learned in the desert for 32 years was enough raw material for 103 books on psychology--cheers!

What I learned from my feminazi sisters/feminist bullies was enough psychiatric analysis for a library, see?

The persecution of leftists went on for decades and we sat quietly--up against a tidal wave--but now it's more ok.

Enjoy your new life now, you're protected behind a wall. Maximize your elder moments/don't go back at ALL.

The more young and ethnically diverse the population the more they call for strong man rule: "CAESARISM".

Polls show the under-35s are far more authoritarian than the older [TRULY AMERICANA] generations.

Signs of decay: corruption, overcomplexity, over-taxation, moral degeneracy, migratory pressures at the border.

Moneyed interests use the media to create the illusion that there is consent from the governed, it's their weapon.

Fake news journalists are the officers, the readers are the soldiers and the dirty work spreads from there.

NEW DEMOCRACY RUN BY MEDIA

This new democracy run by media is no different from a plutocracy run by wealthy elites.

Come what may the polarization and tribalization will only increase as will all the other signs of social decay.

They're here, aren't they? Well that's the whole thing, ok?

Thank you Shane, Dick, Jimmy, Danny, Joe, Chris, Alex for my lesson on neurotics and how to keep em out.

When people are angry it's so easy to tell em a lie--building a fire under em and then we all die.

Four years with whiners isn't education--you only come out with opinions, not skills. George Bruno

When feminism is implanted women take on a false self and it's very unbecoming messing us all up.

EquitySpeak: America is all oppression: men against women, Christians against Islam, whites against everyone.

Women must learn that morality doesn't mean to be "nice" but to be RIGHT.

The Alt Right is against the belief that all races, genders and ethnicities are the same and interchangeable.

"Nice" and "polite" are two different things. Nice glazes over, polite has decorum even while telling em off.

Americans are a distinct people--not everyone can fit in. That's a radical position/could get you fired man.

BEWITCHING LIE: NEED WORKS

Every theological cult disparages the cross of Jesus Christ--it somehow was not enough to pay for our sins.

Catholicism does not believe in salvation by grace alone by faith alone thru Christ alone--must add works on.

If you add anything to faith alone you've a different gospel and we should hate aberrant theological cults too.

Again, EVERY cult disparages the cross and status of Jesus Christ.

EVERY cult disparages the cross and status of Jesus Christ but what He said on the cross was IT IS FINISHED.

It's a foolish statement to say "I don't need doctrine and theology, I just love Jesus"--not true, you'll die.

Paul said to the bewitched: "why are you going back to the enslavement of rules, rituals and ceremonies?

It is foolish to be bewitched by the false additions to the gospel and it's useless, empty and boring as hell.

BEWITCHED: THE CROSS IS NOT ENOUGH?

Are you so bewitched as to think the work of the spirit was incomplete? Is it salvation thru flesh you seek?

Why are you so bewitched and going BACK to a system of rules, ceremonies, rituals and get-togethers?

Salvation to the bewitchers is ALWAYS through grace AND works. That's always the bewitching lie of jerks.

Most churches and their leaders are bewitched. They believed in the gospel but ADDED too much.

There is so much confusion in the church it's incredible, sinning against the holiness of God/its boring too.

Paul was heartbroken over the bewitching coming from people wanting popularity, acceptance, a fling.

Fallen: deadness/emptiness of intellect couched in many words but showing no sense, logic or discernment.

it's the sinful neglect of the truth while you sit around socializing/acting superior cuz you go to church.

Neglect of the truth is a mind issue but mostly a heart issue--it's sick to be told His death's not enough too.

They huddle together bewitched and altogether foolish: ignorant of scripture, brutish and fruitless.

A church filled with bewitched people is FOOLISH people without minds nor hearts open to God's truth.

How could you, after seeing Christ crucified, go back to the law? Was the cross unnecessary/insufficient? Paul

THE CROSS SETTLES IT ALL

The cross settles it ALL.

Or was the cross a partial provision, that you have to make up the rest with your works? Paul on this curse.

You are blaspheming the cross and crucifixion but that's what a works system does and it's never enough.

If your salvation requires something of you, then it's not all Christ. What an insult to His pain on the cross.

The cross isn't just a historical event but it goes on and on eternally with its power forgiving sins every hour.

Legalism doesn't pick up where the cross leaves off cuz the cross never leaves off--never done, never stops.

He perfected the believers forever by the ONE offering of Himself. Hebrews 10: 14

The cross lacks nothing. Salvation is thru grace alone thru faith alone and not through works. Eph 2:8-9

If you bring works in Christ will be of no benefit to you. Gal. 5:2

WORKS SEVERS US FROM CHRIST

If you bring works in--justification by law--you've been severed from Christ and fallen from grace. Gal 5: 4.

The TARES were tolerated by the bewitched believers in Galatia--just another sign and we see it in America.

How can you go to a church which is purely social and run by women? A believer avoids a sanctuary of demons.

When they abandoned all works and finally put their trust in the risen Christ they were TRANSFORMED.

Having begun by the spirit, are you REALLY now being perfected by your flesh?

Christ work on the cross IS complete and the law adds nothing to the work of the Holy Spirit, see this.

Salvation by faith and grace alone: you foolish Galatians, you are so bewitched--you are complete in HIM.

BOUNDARIES AND BORDER CONTROL

Instead of complaining about these friends, work it back to the original trauma that molded you to allow em in.

You, the victim/patient did crazy degrading things cuz you were conditioned by your previous systems.

Alcoholic husband is a broken down hedge and instead of a fence he'll let em all in and you've had it.

If you react with horror he'll bond with his friends against you and they love fighting a gender war too.

So you've gotta nip it in the bud and **VET YOUR GUESTS** cuz once they're in your home, you've **HAD IT**.

If you don't show strength and firmness about border control--what they all know--it's a tidal flow.

ALCOHOL THE MORAL DISINHIBITOR

Alcohol lowers your hedge cuz it's a social lubricant to lower companions. Sobriety equals protection.

Alcohol is a moral disinhibitor. It's the same thing: you've become **INFIRM** with lines and boundaries sir.

Wicked men hypnotize women in their homes. That means she let em in--degraded from previous systems.

I had been imposed on/yelled at my whole life. So when you came to the door I let you in, used to strife.

IMPOSED ON BY PREVIOUS SYSTEMS

With repentance you may have to geographically relocate. People don't forget and they don't want you great.

When you get to the new place try not to reminisce lest it's to teach and for that you've got a wealth of memories.

When you get to safety you have PTSD. It's then these memories are released, to digest you must re-see.

I've gotten past being angry with you the imposer and focusing on me--why I'd ever tolerate all that.

When all human decency is lost it's hell on earth we witness and I think back to when things were nice.

You were in a system that spiraled down, that's all. In your new place it's a **FRESH START** like it never happened.

The lady survivor said "If I didn't let him in he'd get in thru my alcoholic husband and I'd had it."

BLOOD-WASHED MEMORY

With washed memory you can think of all the castles you built and fortunes you made, free of this plague.

With memory in the sin state or **PTSD** it's black grime going thru all the strands--no castles just dank, bland.

Once having settled all this--it was just a system that is now broken--you can go on and create fortune.

So am I saying Joyce Meyer should not preach? No she's a motivational speaker who is a Christian.

I went thru horrible things to get this wisdom--it's what happens in humans as God gives back double man.

What is genius? Surplus Potential in Problem Areas. You go thru something, out comes genius--that's what it is.

IT'S WHAT I DO.

I'm trying to see all the things I built with washed memory. Not the crap--Satan's army of demons God zapped.

I'm gonna see God soon and then all this unfortunate miserable fearful sad stuff will be over, just floatin'

I'm not going anywhere, I just wanna stay home. I've done my work, it should stand on it's own. Aunt's advice

Only a masochist or Christian soldier would go on Joy Behar: The View is dense minds/dark hearts.

We don't wanna be NICE or GOOD but RIGHT and firm about this, always tightening our borders not less.

They just wanna hang around but you wanna be free to be. These are drip dry hangers, losers--a human tragedy.

Alcoholic husband can't see them as lower losers so there goes your personal vetting/you'll go thru the ringer.

The more pure your husband the higher the wall will be. That's being a real man--keeping out the freaks.

Don't let em around your stuff cuz we live in a different day and age. They see it, they want it, it's gone/that's all.

It'll feel so good for you to tell the truth again. You've been blocked, labeled, judged for your truth my friend.

Jezebel did it to her husband, she did it to her mother and now she did it to you. See the spirit, eschew.

The carnal woman is sickening and we gotta do something about it. Jezebel is a divider and must be stopped.

JEZEBEL AIN'T SPIRITUAL SHE'S SOCIAL

She's not truly spiritual cuz ego has taken over and it's all about the social which churchists call "GOD" ya know.

It was the evil pagan feminist witch that started all this. She let em in and it was you she disparaged.

You're safe now after a war. It won't happen again so just try to enjoy what life is left, and adore it.

I was at the mercy of a gang of juvenile delinquents and they knew it. Geo-relocated then fenced up.

These people are not above killing. You gotta get this thru your head and face the bloody truth tho' chilling.

We're no longer safe cuz decency kept us safe and immorality spirals down, it doesn't stay the same.

I've done my work but can't control outcomes. That's outside of me, not the important thing, I'm done.

If a writer isn't read what's the use of writing--I guess it's just for me, huh? Or maybe after I leave thee.

What are these words for if they can't even read? I don't know it's just what I do whether or not I care to.

The kinda people you call wonderful are wretched and terrible. What's wrong with you, your friends know.

He was a leak in your boat. Wherever you'd go he'd take the opportunity to make friends with the low.

He was a leak of your self esteem, every time you went in in public he'd made a scene tho' it was subtle you see.

Did I develop a thorny prickly crust? You bet I did and I went inward now every second is mine, a must.

ONE EVENT CHANGES LIFE FOREVER

One event can change your life forever. Like the woman who had a bucket of diarrhea poured over her.

It was a black cloud and nightmare being around you. Can't put my finger on it but will go with my instinct, whew.

The bad marriage was all about him allowing others to impose on me. That was it, a misery.

Anything which diverts our attention away from scripture is opposite to the author of scripture--the enemy.

We need God but He does not need us. Any man who preaches this is preaching a different gospel.

God doesn't need us--He needs His children to stop associating with the bad guys/the pagans/the nuts.

Good ol' boy network: Wants to get legitimacy by having legit people on cuz he's not that on his own.

Relax--it's just something you went thru. These lessons can be very hard and painful but you learned too.

We've won the battle of the inerrancy of God's word but where we've lost it today is it's SUFFICIENCY.

False preachers have a "little god" program--the little god should never be poor nor sick, that's it.

Her girlfriends hated Christina Aguillar for her great voice. She moved and then went on to fame--its classic.

Did she stay stuck in resentments over this? Of course not and neither should you, see it as a lesson phase.

THE LESSONS WERE HARD BUT FORGET EM NOW

The lessons are hard esp. on the Jezebel Spirit. It's infecting half the world so learn it and rise up.

The PTSD most bad is related to the social: what people do to keep you down or just maintain the status quo.

It doesn't matter if she's gone--I had to flush her out. I had to test the waters and she bloody well flunked.

I've experienced most everything you have. We hear things on TV then think back...OMG not that.

From our new vantage points it stinks to high hell. We can't believe it--it helps to know it was the devil.

Borrego Springs was my Ph.D. in the streets. I never saw anything like it--a buncha liberals crowded in together.

Boys from cities are flooding small towns and taking over. I was a victim of this in Borrego Springs 85' Highers.

These guys are now in their fifties and probably have no idea what they put me through [public schools].

The girls from that era were even worse: sluts, imposing Jezebels who brought confusion in our midst.

CHANGED DEMOGRAPHY: NOT SO BIG YOU SEE

Suddenly in the nineties the demography changed. From white boy's gangs to 99% Mexicans.

Now the white boys took on white guilt and overpowering wives and girlfriends and the culture insured it.

The white boys who got away with everything in small towns were now the targets, seen as maggots.

Many went to prison cuz grandma kept confirming their sins and being ever-forgiving and calling it loving.

It wasn't the Mexicans who bothered me it was the white boys without dads whose moms were feminist!

The middle aged feminists were more like witches without moral lines which they passed on to their descendants.

In an effort to be trendy and remain relevant the middle aged feminist makes a fool of herself in self-disgust.

It isn't cute to be a middle aged slut. Tell the youth It's disgusting to boot and will haunt them later too.

What is the highest past time? Studying doctrine and smashing all their false religion contradictions.

GOD WILL HELP YOU NOW. Just call on Him! He will dispel the demons and make you whole again!

THEY CONSIDER THEMSELVES GODS

They consider themselves gods, you're to shut up and obey--only they can determine what you can say.

Driving defensively is knowing the other guy is **NUTS**. The definition of a good driver: riders are **RELAXED**.

Fake meats are toxic sludge, trendy but truly intended to replace meat that you love way too much.

A man is not supposed to talk liberal like a woman--it's embarrassing/destructive but called "lovin".

These creepy youth so far from the truth are gonna lead our country soon: vile, wrong, absurd, uncouth.

Following too close or taking your eyes off the road is lunatic driving and you must **NEVER** go with this guy again.

Bad drivers aren't just dense [non-defensive] but also bullies, subconsciously loving to terrify the riders, it must be.

Grandma knew digestion was not her friend. She was elegant, ripped, svelt, quiet, scholarly, devout.

This constant hyper-partinization of late-night "comedy" is doing nothing but dividing us more in this war.

They calumniously kill the president nightly and for what? To get fans from a rapidly decreasing media, nuts.

It's a Peak Period [PP] for me in the middle of the night. When the herd is asleep I'm higher than a kite.

She ended the old relationship in the same place where she started a new relationship: God or settling for less?

IS HER SILENCE A RUDDER TO CONTROL?

You say something she doesn't like and there is silence. She uses it like a rudder to control what you say.

Female preachers: the more WRONG they are more they yell their sermons and even start pacin'

You're so wrong you YELL your SERMON. Heathen practices OKed and promoted! Tattoos ETC!

A bad driver is threatening to maim or take your life. It's in his hands so your fear of him will turn to hate.

When it comes to theology, sound doctrine and heresy we absolutely ARE to criticize these matters.

They demote God to make him more human then they deify man to make him a god deserving of millions.

Tolerance is not our friend. It's a mindset that has allowed the enemies of the west to get the upper hand.

The extremely liberal Methodist Church's slogan is "open doors, open hearts, open minds": oh my.

WOMEN: THE CHURCHES HAVE FALLEN

Once a church ordains women into their leadership it's just a matter of time before they side into liberalism.

They'll say the bible isn't necessarily true, you can't read it literally for it's impossible, it's all just a morality tale.

Seeker-sensitive churches have false fellowship, holding hands with anyone no matter the heresy.

"Outdated cultural mores": movies/songs made to conform to ever changing social mores of progressivism.

Joel Osteen--top of the seeker-sensitive movement--says 99% of people good but bible says 100% are bad!

There is none righteous, not even one. There is none that does good, not even one. Romans 3: 10-12

The heart is deceitful above all things and is desperately wicked--who can know it? Jeremiah 17: 9

SICK SEEKER-SENSITIVE MOVEMENT

Thus the seeker-sensitive movement misunderstands how depraved people are--that's their stumbling block.

The land under the false preachers [clouds without water] is dry and parched--that's the modern church.

California pride: crime, feces, homelessness, burning cities, illegal alien invasions, censorship, suicide.

New church has boundless credulity to believe anything/everything and thus it's fighting for it's life.

The herd: widespread ignorance, doctrinal confusion, biblical infidelity--of course I wanted to isolate.

Persecution has a way of refining you. I became a total recluse learning about God and the bible too.

Tho' persecution took its toll God restored my youth as he promised to us all in the greatest story ever told.

I learned that if I didn't have boundaries the sinful world would flow right in--always, like a tidal wave.

Once a church ordains women into their leadership it's just a matter of time before they side into liberalism.

NEW CHURCH EAR-TICKLERS AND SOCIALS

We're warned about ear-tickling teachers, doctrines of demons, destructive heresies, perverse teachings.

New Church: myths, commandments of men, speculations, controversial issues, deceitful spirits, worldly fables.

False knowledge, "science", empty philosophy, traditions of men, worldly wisdom, corruption of the word of God.

Suddenly movies, news, discussions and debates bored me to tears and only doctrine/prayer filled the years.

There is nothing more boring than the false church. It degrades to socials and rituals not the true God.

I learned about common pitfalls of all Christians: becoming worldly and accepting heresy/the liberal narrative.

Them thinking Christian was being "nice" or "good", distorting the gospel so easily misunderstood.

Look at your officious invaders as a litter of puppies: of course they wanted in, creating mayhem naturally.

SHEEP'S CLOTHES ARE WHITE

Beware of false prophets in sheep's clothes [dressed in white not evil black] for they are ravenous wolves.

Ever notice how they insist on dressing in white [despite it showing the spots] or pastels to look spiritual?

They refuse to wear black, it's evil. They wear only white cuz that's spiritual-- examples of spiritual voodoo.

What does the color you wear have to do with Christ death to free you/wash you clean of that terrible sin stain?

Ministers, scientists, maestros, classic nighters and maître des wear black so get over it/wear what you want.

The church has so degenerated that people make up what looks spiritual. They play this game, lost ya know.

Avoiding worldly and empty chatter and the opposing arguments of what is falsely called "knowledge."

THE MOST WORTHWHILE PAST TIME

The most worthwhile past time is studying scripture and false heresies subtly introduced since they ruin it.

Paul warned in Acts that perverse men would rise up from the inside and evil from outside with twisted doctrines.

They're like children tossed to and fro by every wind of doctrine. That's why we must teach it to them.

Wolves in sheep's clothing wear "spiritual" white.

To the Christian Center: How can you be a pastor, elder or deacon unless you can sort out truth from error?

We are not only the purveyors of the truth but guardians of it. Guard what has been entrusted to you.

If you don't guard the trust--the true gospel [that IT IS FINISHED] you will stray from the faith: bad day.

Ok, it's finished--does that mean I can sin all I want? No cuz we are washed clean--released from all that.

If you're so perfectly socially adapted how could you interest me? It's just social promiscuity/nutty.

If you're such a ladies man adapting to liberal women you've known why would I be impressed, ya know?

GTH, leave me alone. They have no depth and neither do you. You're on the phone all day and very boring too.

Guard this TREASURE entrusted to you. It's a SACRED trust, a deposit of divine truth: the scriptures.

That's why hearing such gobbledygook hurts us so much. Voodoo, women, TV preachers all making stuff up.

PURE DOCTRINE IS SIMPLE

Pure doctrine is SIMPLE enough for a child to understand but they unnecessarily complicate it for money man.

We not only have this divine treasure but must divide the word correctly so that the truth can be known.

You're under severe judgment in the pulpit by saying what God said when He didn't or gagging what He did say.

They see the signs of coming weather but not signs of the times requiring diligent study of the scriptures.

Their knowledge of weather far exceeds their spiritual discernment based on who they let in to ruin it.

The ability to discern between the true and false is ESSENTIAL for believers, pastors and leaders.

It's SIMPLE: Examine EVERYTHING carefully, hold fast to what is good and abstain from every form of evil.

Test, prove, validate. This is essentially what God does as He discloses and reveals what's been in the dark.

LIGHT TO GUIDE OR BRICK TO CARRY?

Is your church a lamp to guide or a brick to carry? They weigh you down and then you miss God entirely.

Pure doctrine is SIMPLE not overburdened with socials and rituals or complicated with meetings/who ya know.

In a post-truth world, test everything to distinguish what is true from false, right from wrong, good from bad.

Holding fast: means there's no room for reckless faith or gullibility--believing every new thing or the silly.

The discerning power to know what is inherently good/true from what is evil-- inherently so despite superficial.

To not only abstain from ALL forms of evil but also evil IDEAS for they are the most insidious of all.

When God says to abstain from sexual immorality he means all forms, not just less or restrained sir.

ABSTAIN MEANS COMPLETE

The word abstain means COMPLETE, not infrequent sexual immorality like once in a while--shun it with style.

It is truly sickening what the new world expects of women even on the first date--can she overcome bad fate?

Can she be a true daughter of God and say "NO!" insisting on total chastity until that day she knows?

The new type of pastor committed adultery twice, wears jeans with holes to preach and has tattoos. P-U.

When you find any doctrine or scheme that is EVIL because it isn't TRUE then turn away from it.

Just cuz someone comes to your door you don't let him in. Your mind is the same thing: guard it wisely friend.

I am not concerned with what people think of me. My responsibility is to God not caving to desires of peeps.

Preach in season or out of season--meaning all the time. Point out half-truths, deceptions, lies of Satan.

PERVERSIONS OF TRUTH IS MOST WICKED

The worst form of wickedness is perversions of the truth. Richard Lensky

Because he never had a home he didn't realize the sanctity of YOUR home so don't be dumb and stay alone.

He came into your home and brought evil spirits with him and this is why you went into a deep depression.

Jezebel came into your home and stirred deep divisions while she put you down--reason for depression.

Many look on these perversions with indifference or see them as harmless. No, it's a mess, life or death.

Perversion of the truth is evil: poisonous, destructive, damaging tho' dressed in sheep's clothing.

Abstain from ALL FORMS means any appearance, any inkling, any reason to make em think that way.

Any species, sort or category. Anything which reminds or symbolizes and especially anyone who thinks that way.

People are into your stuff. They want it and will wait till you die to come get it. Fiddler on Roof--the end.

It's the DEVIL who drops things into your mind. It's his playground so you must control it/draw a line.

If the mentally ill or morally debased is let into your home it's the beginning of the end--it's a spirit my friend.

SEXUAL IMMORALITY IS WORST

Men talking women into sex saying it's a "contract" cuz she slipped once and then she gets sick and he rejects.

Don't drink alcohol or you may slip into sex. But that's false doctrine: have a little wine the scripture says.

I see a long welcoming highway in front of me with bright lights all around. It's like a destiny day/I'm glowin'.

With all those people you are locked in man. They talk about you, every little thing and it comes back.

I felt so locked in a small town I'd a done anything to escape and I found a desert wilderness cabin.

INVASIONS OF THE FALSE CHURCH

Then the churches found me/started driving me crazy with falsehood seeking to "save" me but I found Thee.

There was no talk of Jesus but only their apostles or church business or the latest gossip/socials.

Their get-togethers were more like pagan bazaars with booths for music and whatever you desire.

Like Eve influenced Adam, we are led astray from the simplicity and purity of devotion to Christ.

Are you ok with it when you hear a different gospel, a different Jesus? Or does it terrify you, as it should?

The lack of discernment in the truth shows up in so many ways along with unsaved people thinking they're saved.

The biggest reason for the great revivals was churches filled with unconverted people.

Jonathan Edwards was thrown out of his church cuz he wanted to save the Lord's Table for true believers.

You can't bring discernment into an environment that won't tolerate absolutes, discrimination, conviction, dogma.

They hate dogma cuz it divides. They don't want anything threatening their Do As Thou Wilt past times.

MUST HAVE DOCTRINAL CLARITY/CONVICTION

Causes were trends becoming norms: Discernment can't combine with a lack of doctrinal clarity/conviction.

Why did doctrinal conviction die out? It was an obstruction [gets in the way] to pragmatism which took over.

They validate the unbeliever's resentment of the gospel that way--by removing the parts he resents, ok?

And then if you try to re-introduce doctrinal clarity he says you did a bait and switch: you've hit a giant glitch.

In a Post-Truth World they assault any conviction, doctrinal clarity, absolute truth or dogma of reality.

Opposition will decrease if you stay silent on anything that offends the sinner but truth/discernment is lost.

The culture can't think antithetically [true or false, wrong vs. right]. it's a spectrum of shades of grey/no wrongs.

Worldly thinkers don't wanna think in black and white. It makes them uncomfortable, they see it as a blight.

From the Garden to Heaven or Hell God always sets forth TWO ways: saved or lost, God's people or the world.

There is the narrow way or the wide way. One leads to eternal bliss and the other to eternal death.

DEVELOP THE ANTITHETICAL MENTALITY

There are those who are against and those with us. Life or death, truth or falsehood, Kingdom of God or Satan.

There is love and hate, spiritual wisdom and wisdom of the world. The post-truth genre can't think in these terms.

They want shades of grey, not rigid dichotomies. And I feel sorry for them cuz life degrades but not for me.

Instead of saying "no alcohol" they say "yah but it's ok to have a beer once in awhile". That's always their style.

Even the Hebrew language reveals antithesis in scriptural poetry and proverbs--it's antithetical in nature.

Every day in everything we do we must choose God's way or man's way. We need conviction/clarity daily.

In the old days God's people were constantly encouraged to develop an antithetical mentality, but not today.

Discernment only thrives where there's a black and white, antithetical mentality. Therefore it is gone, truly.

Now its just Image and influence: Build an image of love and niceness, make everyone comfortable and happy.

If you're seeking prestige in our culture you'll lose the will to discern and discriminate: yes or no, black or white.

BLURRED LINES IS THE FEMINIZATION OF THE CHURCH

This loss of discernment and certainty is the feminization of the church. It's more like women think: blurry.

Blurred lines and ambiguity shows the church has lost its manliness. It's become empty and meaningless.

Warnings and opposition to error were essential parts of any commitment to the bible but now it's "love".

The prevailing attitude puts "love first" and calls any argument over doctrine "unChristian", cursed.

The person standing for truth and discernment is marginalized then fired and penalized.

It's the age of appeasement in the church. Discerning men are called noncooperative, difficult and self-assertive.

Why the church has fallen: lack of conviction, failure to be antithetical, concern with worldly image.

The church has lost its will to terrify and disturb the sinner. That was its function, to restore him much faster.

The new trend is mega-church pastors, self-appointed and untrained handlers of scripture cuz image comes first.

WORLDLY CHATTER AND UNGODLINESS

So much worldly chatter leads to further ungodliness like gangrene. Straying from truth and then misleading.

Lack of discernment is spiritual immaturity. Baby Christians are carried to and fro with every theory.

Discerning man keeps wisdom in view but a fool's eyes wonder to the ends of the earth. Prov 17: 24

Spiritual discernment is the ability to distinguish God from Satan. That wasn't you girl, you let em ALL in.

I can tell sound doctrine from perversion, the latter makes me literally sick. It makes me mad too, what freaks.

When they start spouting "love everybody" and sugarcoated crap like that I know it immediately.

We're to "cry for discernment". That's how important this is so pray every day for it while you're being hit.

SEEK KNOWLEDGE LIKE HIDDEN TREASURE

Seek knowledge like hidden treasures then you will discern and it's the opposite to common knowledge sir.

Where is the place of understanding? Man doesn't know it's value and it can't be bought by the living.

Pray for discernment then follow scripture cuz that's the wisdom from above/follow discerning teachers love.

I love the truth, I love hearing it, I desire it and I love those who preach it. It's the HA-HA Kum-Ba-Yah opposite.

We're to discern--keep the bad or false OUT. Not be inclusive, what the world calls "loving" but is not.

YOU are the hope of the world because you can discern the truth. Pray for boldness to proclaim it too.

There are churches that aren't churches, pastors who aren't pastors and "Christians" or aren't either man.

There are only two possible options: the narrow gate to heaven, the wide gate to hell and no middle.

Narrow gate is hard to find/hard to go through. I can attest to this, it meant isolation and being called a "shrew".

I was always drawing lines and boundaries, it was No, No, No! They want yes to everything, going so low.

Narrow: denial of self, recognition of sin, full repentance, submission to Christ to obey no matter what the cost.

It's hard to act on this due to the love of self and love of sin which is natural to the sinner from where he's been.

WAY TO HEAVEN IS APART FROM THE CROWD

The true way to heaven is hard to find, apart from the crowd, naked of status symbols, penitent, all alone.

Most religious people are on the broad road and there's plenty of false prophets around to fool and goad.

These false prophets, religious leaders and representatives of Christ and God are really agents of Satan.

They lead people on a road marked "heaven" but is really hell. They look nice/drive a nice car but smell.

They spend fortunes on plastic surgery cuz everyone's looking at em and it works in a Dionysian generation.

It's called the "Judas tragedy" where you hang around Jesus but belong to Satan--where you been?

Whole churches can be deceived about their true spiritual condition. Despite voiced intentions it's all a sham.

God was speaking here to fastidiously religious people, not a buncha losers. The former are the most closed sir.

These Pharisees were obsessed with religion, that's a fact. It ran thru all facets of life--as religious as one can get.

Totally religious and yet NO relationship to God or Christ. Just to the church members, desiring to impress.

Religious but lost, on wrong road. Socially embossed but not a prince just a toad. Socially adapted/not bold.

They have a form of godliness without the reality of it. All they do is gossip about the misfit like they're above it.

Self-deception is everywhere: somehow connected to "Jesus/God" but devoid of divine life/being awed.

Without any knowledge of God or salvation at all. Acceptance of anything/everything of the world.

SHALLOW GOSPEL GOES TO HELL

Deceived souls in churches on the "Jesus trip" thinking all is well but are workers of "loving" lawlessness.

What a shock to think you're on the way to heaven but to find out you're in hell--that's happening now.

Why it happens: a superficial understanding of the gospel dominates Christiandom/no one rebukes it hon'

A failure to understand the true terms of the gospel: salvation and saving faith, repenting each day.

Most churches now have a weak, shallow, superficial, trivialized, emotionalized, psychologized gospel.

Most Christians in the pew could not give you a meaningful explanation of the great doctrines of redemption.

They don't know their spiritual condition cuz they don't even know what saving faith and the gospel is.

You'd think someone who debunks error and propagates truth would be a hero, but is seen as an anti-hero.

The truth-teller is treading on people's feelings, invading the comfort level of their tolerances, being divisive.

Ignorant of the gospel: Just want people's approval, going to all the socials but never mentioning truth ya know.

I walked into the church and was overwhelmed with another gospel, just a social, falsehood of y'all.

To preach the true gospel today is engaging in more warfare than to preach it to the godless world.

The false church is all rituals or socials.

They are lured into deception BECAUSE they know not the gospel--made to feel good about any situation at all.

SHALLOW AFFIRMATIONS

They are affirmed by the mere shallow desire to be a Christian. If you just pray this prayer, you're in.

You'll be "certified" but if you come to the altar, doubly-certified. If you stick to boring meetings, bonafide.

If you go to the socials and make friends with everyone, you're totally a Christian to them--what folly friends!

They pick Mr. and Mrs. Popularity as their "elder team"--it's all about status and social acceptance you see.

Say the right things, have the correct emotional responses to the events--you get the point, it's not about Jesus.

According to the church God and Jesus loves Mrs. Social Charm the best. This is by far the biggest scamfest.

What about the shy introvert who just loves God? He's not accepted and should learn better to get along.

KAREN'S HEALTHY CANDIES

It's the Breakfast-Only Plan. What I can handle ONCE in the morning I could never handle later/bummer.

So far it's just for family and friends but the theory is what even a child can understand, just do it man.

Karen's Healthy Candies: Any inferior food eaten previously detoxes out [sick] so stop eating it hick.

My new baking friends know about nutmeg, orange peel, lemon twist, cloves and they know where it all goes.

Grandma made candies and we never got fat just healthier due to her baking with things like saffron and all that.

CANDY HEALERS

They knew just how to balance the nutmeg, just where we need a hint of orange. They knew the errors to avoid.

I'm hungry to know all this but don't wanna read a book. I'm looking for traditional female wisdom we forsook.

It should be easy if we can get kids eating traditional candy which was God's food on the earth for us, truly.

The way the youth are taught they're not only totally debauched but selfish, loud and arrogant fops.

My bars: dates, raisins, nuts, coconut flakes, dried fruit--held together by melted nutbutter/honey/chocolate.

These are energy bars with all God's ingredients and wow--Ray came alive suddenly with so little, and he's full.

Energy bars are totally customizable using all natural ingredients--I made a year's worth for food storage.

I've reached the point where cooking and eating is a terrible chore--my energy bars are the answer.

Nuts, honey, fruit, coconut are paleo superfoods. If organic you got all bases covered, go forward fast dudes.

I can't eat, I have no interest in food, it's lost all logic for me--but I CAN and WILL eat my bars for energy.

I dropped a couple grand on dried fruits, honeys, chocolates, coconut products & nuts for basement.

Now I'll make our energy bars once a month or six times a year--how simple and clear, it's perfect dear.

I'm sick of food preparation yet I feel responsible for my family's nutrition as a woman, so this is my solution.

Pomegranate cookies, raspberry and macadamia cookies, papaya and almond chocolate cookies--with the BEST.

NUTS, COCONUT, FRUIT, SUPERFOODS, CACAO

These energy bars produce instant satiety--it's the "aliesthenic hunger turnoff": after just one [half].

Ray will be getting fruit and other great superfoods, in the bars. Things he wouldn't usually, like hibiscus flowers.

My energy bars are hyper-nutrition/calories in a small space, at last I know I'm doing right by my mate.

One-half energy bar and I am SO FULL. High nutrition, low mass = hunger turns off immediately, how wonderful.

How inefficient: cooking in a disaster. The home-made [superior materials] energy bars are the answer.

All my food storage was starches before. No, no, no--that's the last staff, use fruits/nuts for your bars.

Dessert Superfoods--nuts, coconut, honey/maple, fruits-- for beauty or if stressed: "desserts" spelled backwards.

Karen's Energy Bars: The varieties are endless and it's all incredibly micro-nutritious and delicious.

Ate half a bar and was so satiated I couldn't eat all day. Max nutrition in low mass = aliesthenic hunger turn off.

In the past, candy was a healthy thing: chocolate, nuts, coconut, honey, nut-butters: energy/laxative.

Put em altogether and what do you get: God's energy in what He made combined with incredibly delicious flavor.

CANDY IS A GOOD THING AGAIN

Key to weight loss: Have a big breakfast, the sun for lunch and then just skip dinner--lose pounds, a bunch.

Like living in a painting: Arizona Strip is polygamy-friendly FLDS environment, everything is orderly and quiet.

Searched for my slimfit open front tuxedo jacket and they're ALL polyester: on my best day I'll be sick.

At 75 Joyce Meyer is her most beautiful/powerful--that's how aging should be and was traditionally, before now.

I may die by not eating meat but I'd rather have Karen's Healthy Candy.

From the beginning music made me so happy. There was no gossiping, imposing, bothering or triangulating.

Music doesn't bother me like people yet it comforts me as a friend and it happens instantly every time it's on.

With music there's no fighting back or using me for something. It doesn't talk it just goes real deep.

The world's best musicians may be very lonely, practicing 6 hours a day. To succeed greatly it's a price we pay.

I was always very studious and had to fight for the right to work in privacy which brought ridicule from the lazy.

I get gut aches from nuts or corn tortillas, my favorites. These poke holes in the gut bringing on acid reflux.

New routine: European movies, Joyce Meyers heavily and my Karen's Healthy Candies with infinite recipes.

Yesterday I ate right. Had I not I may be detoxing now--and that means ACID REFLUX day and night.

COLON CLEANSING CANDY

Everyone knows they feel better after a thorough evacuation. Karen's Healthy Candy is the solution.

It's been 18 hours fasting now. I've gotta pizza waiting for my breakfast but I'm so high I'm gonna extend it, wow.

Expect major colon detox from Karen's Healthy Candies: fruits, raisins, dates, nuts, coconut, honey, superfoods.

The more you detox [SCRAPE] the colon the less hunger the next mornin' and the more energy you got goin'.

Honey, I want only the essential--the quintessential--not superfluity. I want elegance not all this shit, truly.

Who'd guess I'd find my home on an Acid Reflux Group on Facebook or as a healthy candymaker? I am blessed.

We've bought the big freezers and the raw materials for our Karen's Healthy Candy [KHC] operation startin'

Pizza or bacon are both ok if eaten in the morning but in the aft, forget sleeping for all the acid and burping.

With daily fasting the hip bumps which your husband calls feminine will gradually decrease in size. <sigh>

What I learned from first failure: A candy is not a cupcake. Thick is too heavy--stick to brittles, pralines, thin = ok.

You have your dry mixture and your melt {caramel cement]--don't make the dry mixture moist or it's not like that.

Putting my healthy candies in the blended smoothie makes it more robust for both breakfast AND lunch.

I'm just not into eating anymore, I find it a tedious chore--a nutritionally-dense candy-smoothie is the answer.

MEAL REPLACEMENT PAR EXCELLENCE

My candy smoothie is a meal replacement par excellence and most superior, efficacious and latest science.

I lost confidence in the taste of my candies then realized they went in smoothies so don't have to be finicky.

Two recipes today: Apple Macadamia Acai and Apricot Pecan Pomegranate both with chocolate, wow.

My neighbors living on smoothies with my candies blended in and they're higher/fuller than they've ever been.

We didn't even eat the pizza, gave it to the dogs--our tastes are unleveled cuz the system's unclogged.

Take my candy smoothie into old folk's homes and mental hospitals. You'll see rejuvenations like a miracle.

Put the candy in the blender with frozen mangos. It makes a refreshing drink of dense nutrition and nothing else.

It's the latest science about what constitutes micro-nutrition and includes superfoods to get slim.

It works mechanically in the pipes-and-tubes concept of anatomy: the fruit dissolves/nuts scrape colon neatly.

DESSERTS SPELLED BACKWARDS: STRESSED

I would call these "Dessert Superfoods" or "Bible Desserts" or Historical Desserts. Spelled backwards: stressed.

I have much less stress now, in digestion [it auto-digests immediately], acid reflux or insomnia nightly.

God doesn't want me to suffer with acid reflux, bubbles, burping and pain and gave me the answer after I prayed.

Why would a Christian bake a carrot cake packed with crap? Why wouldn't he just use what God made?

Once I realized acid reflux is common and joined others addressing our common pain, end of problem.

My only tattoos will be my eyebrows. They are permanent and will look very professional [but Ray says no]

I can't graze all day, that's not gonna work. I need ONE digestive burn cuz energy's a budget: fast to learn.

In our mango smoothie this morning I put Red Maca and Acai and right now we're higher than a kite.

Ray loves my smoothies and isn't hungry all day from the aliesthenic hunger-turnoff from nutrient-dense foods.

Some can only eat once a day cuz it's genetic. They have the energy for one digestive burn but two wreaks havoc.

My grandmother was a OMADer from a kink in her colon. One can get thru but the second is acid reflux man.

The Eat-Bugs/insects thing is all about assaulting western culture. They wanna ban meat by taxing it for sure.

Grandma had the same problem, called a "kink in her colon" which meant one meal a day, never two.

She had the digestive burn for one meal but not two lest her body flood with acid reflux from autoimmune.

Grandma was skinny as a rail just for survival. We all gotta eat but to have all that superfluous flesh is lethal.

My doctors are astounded I prefer to eat one meal to control my acid reflux and not take their meds.

God took this disability [of acid pain since birth] and turned it into glory with my iron will to victory.

ACID REFLUX IS KARMA FOR EARLY ERROR

You gotta jettison superfluous flesh to deal with the constant chemicals and crap invading, trash.

Healthy candies in the morning: BINGO. Same candies in the late afternoon: acid burn, choking, vertigo.

I see people loading up for dinner and can't believe it. Aren't they gonna choke and be in pain all night?

Yes, God took my disability and turned it all around to good. It's a glorification to do what others won't.

God took my disability and turned it all around to good. It's a glorification to do what others won't or could.

Since acid reflux is also a reaction to chemicals, digestion in the afternoon adds to total load/sick all night.

FAST TO BALANCE TOTAL LOAD

My country neighbors burn trash in the aft. I must fast then to balance the load--you must always calculate.

If I go to town in my new car smell, I must stay home the next day to balance the load thru time as well.

If I get hungry in the aft I'll have a few pieces of dried fruit but that's all lest' I wanna be in pain later on.

Whatever you do as a youth will come back later to haunt you and early anorexia does it thru acid reflux.

I have no more food demons so fasting all day is no sweat. It's so easy too--breakfast only and hubby is svelt.

Fast food isn't "meat" it's mostly oil and wheat.

I learned long ago digestion was not my friend, it just raised total load on immune system: OMAD man.

Many pizzas aren't real cheese. You're being glued up inside and it's from chemicals/fillers you don't see.

KAREN KELLOCK PH.D.

M.S. Political Science, San Diego State. Ph.D. in Psychology, University of California Irvine. Postdoctoral: UCI School of Medicine, Dept. of Psychiatry [NIMH Grants]. Developed the Debris Theory of Disease, a theory of system pathology in 120 books and 22 textbooks for the general public. The theory has a general formula: All disease is obstruction, all recovery is elimination, all success is attraction. The three obstructions are people, habit and food. Remove obstruction and snap to your goals, waiting in the wings.